How to Save a Surgeon

Thomas Blee, MD

with Brian Scott

9 FOOT VOICE

www.9footvoice.com

Cover design by Brittany Kalscheur
www.brittanykalscheur.com

ISBN: 978-0-9968432-2-5

To Mom and Dad.
Thank you for all you have done for me.
Everything is going to be just fine.
I love you both.

Holy and gracious God,

Bless the hands which hold this book, that they may do your work. Bless the eyes which scan these pages, that they may seek Your face. Bless the lips which quietly read along, that they might share Your good news. And bless the souls which understand these words, that we may belong entirely to You.

In Jesus' name, Amen.

Contents

Forward

I had the opportunity to witness a man completely broken and rebuilt. It was a harsh cold reality that I will remember the rest of my life. I watched this surgeon come down from his tower and walk amongst people. I witnessed unselfish compassion given to the 'least of these' while the pain of every day living became a monumental task for the man that I lovingly call 'Doc.'

I recall our first meeting came through the request of a good friend of mine. In my community, if a doctor asks to meet with you, you say, "Yes!" I expected royalty to come walking through the door, but in came a very gracious man who treated me like I was something special. He wanted my help with the kids which society sometimes wishes did not exist: gang bangers, felons, drug addicts and suicidal youth from the inner city; those who are part of the least, the last and the lost.

He felt that they had value and deserved a chance to live. He hoped they could be reached in the space that surgeons create after they save a person's life. He wanted my gang and street credibility to work with him and become a support network for their complete recovery. He envisioned a healthy and vibrant transformation for these broken children. He referred to it as LIFEteam.

But something remarkable happened along the way. His life began to completely fall apart right before my eyes. He almost lost his license even though he had done nothing wrong. He lost his marriage. His relationships with family and friends were tested. He went to jail. He was broken in half emotionally. In the midst of a storm which would have destroyed most of us he reached out to his patients in a way that provided miraculous healing. He offered something you cannot receive in a hospital. He became a hope dealer to the kids he served, allowing them access to his personal life. He would take them to lunch or invite them to Thanksgiving dinners at his sister's house. He personally reached out with the warmth of friendship to me as we worked together to help kids that the world had turned their back on.

During this time we had long conversations about faith. We prayed a lot. We hoped a lot. He always kept these kids as his first priority. In his most broken point he himself made a miraculous recovery: he saved a surgeon. He trusted the things he was saying to the kids, that there is a GOD and He is alive and working on their behalf. I witnessed him become a truly complete surgeon that not just operates in the operating room but in his own life. I witnessed pride disappear and compassion take its place.

Not only should surgeons read this but all people in the medical profession and healing services. This is transformation in its purest form. And being a man that did not have a father I witnessed the love he has for his sons Nick and Jack and through many conversations got to understand what a father's love means.

Read this book. There is a special message for you.

- John Turnipseed

Author of <u>Bloodline</u> and executive vice-president of Urban Ventures in Minneapolis, Minnesota.

Prologue

It was about seven at night, only a few hours into my shift, and my pager sounded like a casino slot machine. As I hurried to the trauma bay, I passed through the emergency room. Two people were receiving CPR and one was getting intubated, so there were three active cardiac arrests. In the hallway, one young man was barfing while an older lady screamed. A helicopter was on its way with a woman who'd been thrown from the back of a four wheeler. The trauma team was assembling and as we prepped for her arrival we received word that a child was being rushed to us after falling out a window. It was chaos, but with a subtle structure underneath - an utterly impossible symphony of human misery and expert care.

I have a chair I like to use when things get this way. My colleagues will often laugh at me, but before the patients arrive, before the frenzy of decisions, actions and consequences, I take a moment and sit. And in that chair I pray, "God, thanks for being here. Thanks for this team. Thanks for a hospital where people trust us. God, direct us, guide us, and heal us. When this mess settles down tonight, give everyone peace." Around me there were family members screaming and crying and dropping to the floor. The helicopter was landing; it was almost time to go to work, but first I prayed again, "Give them peace, God. There's such chaos out there. Could you fire up your angels and calm some of it down?"

Our patients arrived and we leapt into action - but then an ambulance drove up with the first victim of a shooting. The scene, according to the EMTs, had been a bloody mess. They didn't know how many more could be hurt and coming our way. As we listened, a man started barfing and it splashed on my shoes. In that moment I couldn't help thinking: I want my chair back.

Where could anyone see impossible healing in the midst of this symphony of chaos? Every shift, I am surrounded by despair, death, and disease, but still the answer is simple: We see it in the Impossible Healer. He's got us. He is a steady candle in the darkest valley - even in the canyon of death. When things fall apart we look for Jesus. He is the way, the truth, and the light.

Part One:

Caitlyn

Empty Tank

I met José outside the trauma bay and told him what I knew: The patient had been t-boned by a dump truck as she crossed a highway on her way to high school. The truck was going sixty and had no time to brake before slamming into her driver's side door. Somehow the young woman - her name was Caitlyn - had survived the initial impact, but she needed more immediate care than the local hospital could offer.

It was one of those days in early May when the radar screen was full of color - non-stop drizzle with bursts of high wind and lightning. This meant flying wasn't an option so she had to make the trip to our hospital in the back of an ambulance. It's a sixty-five minute trip by car. They made it in forty-two.

José was my physician's assistant and a trusted friend. When I finished my report, I told him, "Start praying now."

He answered, "I already am."

The ambulance rolled in and the rest of our team assembled. The transport crew gave their report, "We haven't had a blood pressure most of the ride. The best we had was sixty over nothing - and that was twenty minutes ago."

Sixty over nothing is essentially incompatible with life - and if someone's heart stops after a blunt trauma, they have less than a half of one percent chance at survival. We all studied Caitlyn for a moment. She had been hit by a dump truck, which was about as blunt a trauma as one could imagine. She had minimal cardiac activity so even if her heart was beating it hadn't been circulating blood properly.

The emergency medicine attending said, "Do we call this?"

It was a fair question. For two hours, there had been a critical shortage of blood feeding Caitlyn's brain, liver and kidneys. The situation appeared hopeless. José, however, saw something the rest of us did not.

"She's not dead," he said.

I looked again. She should be dead according to the data, but José could be right. Still, it was a difficult call. Even if her heart were currently beating - which it wasn't - she had no realistic chance of survival. To counter that, all José had was little more than a gut feeling. It was an impossible decision but it was mine to make.

I believe in prayer. When my trauma pager went off, I prayed. When my team assembled, I prayed. When the transport arrived, I prayed. Here again in the spare moments before action was necessary, I prayed, "God, this is in your hands. Guide our work and help us make the right choices." Then I said to my team, "She has an empty tank, but she's not dead. Let's start CPR."

Once the decision had been made, my trauma team wasted no time. We threw a CPR machine on her, which was essentially a suction cup attached to a pump. As that started, the nurses tried to insert an IV but they couldn't find any legitimate veins, so we drilled two lines into her shins and one into her shoulder. We hung units of blood as we hurried to the operating room; nurses were squeezing it into her as they ran alongside the gurney. It was a mad race against time to fill her gas tank.

The anesthesiologist met us in the operating room. He took one look at Caitlyn and shook his head in disbelief. "Tom," he said. "What the hell?"

I said, "We're doing CPR."

"But why? This is blunt trauma."

"Because she's still with us," I said. "Let's go." José had had a gut feeling and now so did I. Maybe the data didn't support it, but we could see she was still fighting for her life.

The nurses draped her, the anesthesia crew inserted another line in her neck, and we brought in more coolers of blood. We didn't have the time to follow our usual process for prepping a patient's belly, so they dumped an antiseptic called Betadine on her skin as we put on our protective garb and headlights. All of this - from trauma bay to operating room - took a matter of minutes. I grabbed a knife and in one swat full thickness I unzipped her from stem to stern.

The CPR machine kept pounding away. Blood splashed from the incision; it poured off the table, quickly soaking us from our shoes to our kneecaps. To get upstream of the damage, I grabbed her aorta. It is the main vessel coming off the heart and it supplies everything in the belly. I gripped high and pushed it against her spine, squeezing like I was kinking a hose. In my other hand I held her badly damaged spleen. As I did this, one of my residents worked in her pelvis, slamming absorbent packs against bones so ripped up they oozed blood. When the worst of the bleeding stopped, we started to fill her tank. For a few long moments there was nothing to do but wait. I spent the time in quiet prayer, asking God to do the impossible and heal this broken young woman.

Blue Coolers

Caitlyn had to have blood; nothing else would do. Every attempt to create artificial blood in a laboratory has failed. We have components like plasma and platelets, but these cannot do the whole job. We could stuff seven more bags of clear fluid into her body but that would only kill her faster.

The blood comes in hard-sided blue coolers. In the mayhem of pounding lines and running for the operating room, someone is always shouting, "Who's got the cooler?" and "How much volume do we have?" In the middle of almost every maneuver in a trauma surgery, I'm holding on tight to an artery or an organ until we can get the patient's blood to a comfortable level. If I loosen my grip, the patient will bleed out and die.

"When was the blood there?" It is our first question when we review a situation, and - though the system to match the right blood to the right patient is complex - the process must take less than five minutes. Each second is critical and there is no substitute - there is no plan B. Nothing else in the room can help. There is no fluid more necessary to life.

To some it may at first seem strange, but it is no cosmic accident that the reign of Christ is marked by blood. Jesus could have come into our world with declarations of power, and an army of angels. Instead, he entered into the world as we all do, in the mess of blood and fear and pain of childbirth - and to a poor girl in the backwater section of a conquered nation. After only a few years of prominent ministry, he was arrested. Jesus' time on earth could have culminated with a coronation in front of a heavenly choir, instead it ended with blood: nails pounded through his flesh and a spear piercing his side.

There is no fluid more necessary to life. In our flesh, we need it to survive and to heal. In Christ, it is no different: his blood gives us life. As Paul told the people of Ephesus, "In him we have redemption through his blood, the forgiveness of sins, in accordance with the riches of God's grace."[1]

We have to have blood to live and to heal - both on this earth and into eternity.

---

1   Ephesians 1:7

Buzzing Silence

Caitlyn's problem came down to this: her gas tank was empty. We needed to stop the bleeding and fill her back up with blood. In the spring of 2014 I was in a similar situation, but it wasn't my body that was bleeding out. No, I was physically healthy, but my spirit was broken. I had finally run dry and - though I didn't know it yet - I needed the blood of Jesus to fill me up. There was no substitute. There was no plan B. Nothing else but the real thing would do.

It was a Saturday, the First of March, and I sat home alone in what we called the white room; it's a little office with windows facing the front yard. My life was right where I wanted it to be except I was absolutely miserable. I had all the things I thought I needed, but I was hollow. I kept working through my options as a man to muscle through the pain, but none of them offered hope. I thought if I worked harder I'd be happier. If I bought more I'd be at peace. But I was doing nothing but chasing after the wind.

I am a surgeon. I fix people. At the time, I thought I was

the ultimate healer, yet here was a crisis in the heart of my life and I had no idea how to repair it. I couldn't make it better; and if I couldn't do it, I didn't know where to turn.

The problem went as far back as I could remember. Both my parents are healthier now, but my mother was an alcoholic and my father could be described as a workaholic. They both, in their way, did what they thought needed to be done to survive and provide for their children, but our house was often filled with chaos. As a child I never knew what I would find when I came home. The car might be parked on the front lawn. Or I might have to call my grandmother in tears because I was so young I mistook passed-out for dead. Weeks would go by before anyone checked in on us. Ultimately, I coped by sneaking away by myself to my bedroom. It felt safer on my own. There, I learned a terrible lesson: You can trust no one but yourself.

In one way, this became a blessing. In the quiet of my bedroom, I learned to study for long hours which was an essential skill for success in medical school. My childhood, as rough as it was, gave me the toolbox I needed to eventually become a surgeon.

In the operating room, I found both a great deal of satisfaction and a new place to hide. There, no one could touch me. People could ding me on my opinions, on my choices, on anything else about me, but as a surgeon I was safe. It became my entire identity. A source of untouchable pride, it became a comfortable barrier between me and those around me, between me and God, between me and the chaos of daily life.

There is an old joke: What's the difference between God and a surgeon? The answer: God doesn't think he's a surgeon. I felt safe retreating behind my scrubs - as a surgeon,

I was the one in control - but it came with an unbearable responsibility: Every outcome, both good and bad, was dropped on top of me.

For a long time, I functioned at a high level while silently collapsing under the weight of each day's decisions. After a shift I'd slump home to stare at the ceiling late into the night, dwelling on the smallest mistakes, listing all the ways I had gone wrong. It was a form of introverted arrogance which said: I am the final word on healing. The patient's fate - life, death or anything in between - is entirely dependent on me.

I've seen colleagues struggling under similar burdens smother their feelings with booze and drugs, then watch numbly as their families fall apart. Me, I retreated deeper into myself, just as I did when I was a child. I couldn't get past the feeling of shame and failure so I shut down and closed off. I went nearly mute.

An external silence fell around me, but there was nothing but clanging noise inside my head. It was an irritating, buzzing emptiness. I tried to unravel in my head how to fix it but my thoughts were loose and wild. I could only cry out, "What do I need to do to get you out of me?"

I didn't know it at the time, but that buzzing in my head was a defense mechanism. It distracted me from this terrifying truth: I was damaged. There was something broken within me and I needed saving. A few stitches and a bandage wasn't going to do it. A little outpatient procedure wouldn't help. No, I was suffering from a mortal wound; I was bleeding out and needed a full transfusion of blood. I needed someone to fill my tank.

And so it was Saturday night, the first of March, and I was home alone in the white room. I knew I needed to talk to someone, but the only person who would listen to me was my sister, Amy, and she always said the same thing. Frankly, I wasn't in the mood to have another Christ-sandwich shoved down my throat.

Still, there was no one else. So even though it was late, after ten o'clock, I dialed her number knowing she would answer. She said hello with a sigh, as exhausted by this recurring conversation as I was. A small part of me fought to put on a show of strength but the sobbing started before I spoke a full sentence. I was utterly confused. It didn't make sense. I was a successful surgeon. I had all this stuff. Why was my marriage falling apart? Why was I miserable?

She said, "How many more times do you want to make this call? Why don't you try something different?"

"Don't bother." I wiped my eyes on my sleeve. "I know what you're going to say."

She said it softly, as she had a hundred times before. "Tom, you might want to get to know Jesus."

"You've been saying that for years and it's nuts."

"What else do you have?"

The question hurt. I was empty and we both knew it. I said, "I don't have anything."

"You have nothing, Tom. You might as well try."

Our conversation trailed off and my sister, I'm sure, went to bed and was soon sound asleep. But I didn't move. I sank into the little couch in that white room and for a long time stared at nothing. The silence was pounding. The whole house was dark except for the soft light of the street lamps pouring through the windows. Some stubborn part of me continued to resist. It was nuts, I thought - and stupid. Jesus couldn't possibly be the answer to anything outside a Sunday School lesson.

It was late. I was about to head upstairs to spend another mostly sleepless night studying the ceiling - but I couldn't get myself off the couch. Why should I bother? Nothing would be different in the morning. I had nothing left. I was empty. My sister was right: there were no other options. Finally, knowing full well it was absurd, I decided it couldn't hurt to at least give this Jesus a chance.

I muttered something like, "Forget it," and started to pray - but after barely closing my eyes I figured I might as well get on my knees and do the thing properly. I twisted off the couch and lowered myself into the carpet.

It hurt. It felt like I was giving up. It felt like the end of me, but still I prayed. I didn't know how to start so I simply said, "All right. Jesus, I don't know a thing about you." If I was going to do this, I might as well be honest, so I confessed, "I don't even believe you exist. I can't tell when you've ever shown up in my life, you or your Father. But here I am coming to you right now. I am lost and I need help."

I am a scientist and a surgeon. As a scientist I could explain God away. As a surgeon I have minutes at most to make a decision. So I said, "You have about five minutes to show me that you're even here, that you exist. Otherwise I'm out." Then I grew quiet. I fully expected to be disappointed. I expected to soon get off my knees, shake the crazy from my head, and go on being miserable. I expected confirmation that I was right all along and my sister was a nut.

For years I had been hiding behind that buzzing silence. It emanated from a gaping hole within me which only grew bigger no matter what I did. I don't know how long I was on my knees, a minute or two, but it wasn't long before the silence changed. It was so dead quiet in my house I could hear my heart beat in my eardrums - but the buzzing silence stopped expanding out.

In its place I began to feel a presence. In the stillness of that dark room - and for the first time in as long as I could remember - I did not feel alone. On my knees after my prayer, I felt a wholeness. It was as if God were saying, "I'm here. I'm around you. Your emptiness is full."

Neon Lights

I got up off my knees and felt different. Lighter. I could breathe better, like a weight had been removed from my chest. But I was also confused. I had no idea what I was supposed to do next. None of my training had prepared me for Jesus.

I live in a small town, I needed something, and it was late - so I went to the only place that would still be open: Walmart. It was close to midnight when I walked past the greeter. I had no idea what I was looking for or where to find it, but I only made it a few steps before stumbling upon a display of Bibles. They were on sale and in large print - which was perfect for my bad eyes. I thumbed through one and the words of Jesus were all printed in red. God couldn't have been more obvious if he put a giant arrow with the words "Get one of these, Tom!" in neon lights.

I hurried home, tore the plastic wrapping from my new Bible, then puzzled out where to start. The New Testament is Jesus, I reasoned, so I'll start there. The pages crinkled as I opened to the book of Matthew.

I struggled through the list of strange names, then sailed through the next chapter. I kept going, soaking up these stories about Jesus in a way I never had before. It was late, but I didn't want to stop. I would have read through until morning if God hadn't smacked me upside the head.

I was in the fourteenth chapter of Matthew. Jesus had just fed thousands of people and done a bunch of miracles when he decided it was time to go off by himself for awhile to pray. He told his boys, "Get in the boat and I'll meet you later."

Jesus spent the afternoon alone on the mountain talking to his father. Shadows stretched, evening came and a nasty storm started brewing over the lake. From the far shore Jesus knew his boys were freaking out. He wanted to get out there to settle them down, but didn't have a boat. So he did something both simple and impossible: he walked.

When his boys spotted him, they thought he was a ghost. Even though they had just watched him feed 5000 people and had seen him raise a man from the dead, the disciples couldn't believe he was walking on water. It is a familiar trap for people of faith: Even though we know Jesus can do the impossible, we somehow can't believe he would do it for us.

Finally one disciple recognized the water-walker as Jesus and grew excited as only crazy Peter could. He thought, "I need to be where the Lord is - but he isn't getting here fast enough. I don't care if I have to walk on water, I'm heading towards Christ."

Peter cried out, "Call my name!"

Jesus answered, "Peter, come over here."

Peter jumped out of the boat and started walking across the waves. When he was looking at Jesus, he was fine, but when he looked down he realized he was doing something impossible. Humans can't walk on water; he was acting crazy - and as he thought this he started to sink. The storm raged around him, and the sea swelled over his head until water filled his mouth and nose. His life for a moment was in real danger until Jesus grabbed his hand, said, "I've got you," and pulled him up.

When I hit that 'I've got you,' there was a knock-me-down, take-my-breath, piercing silence pounding in my ears. It stopped my reading. The world hushed.

"I've got you," Jesus says. "I have this. I've got it. You're mine." In that moment I knew it was true. I knew I had help. I knew there was something bigger.

I believed.

That night was the start of an incredible journey which has been unlike anything I could have imagined. I've experienced the love of Jesus; I've met amazing people; I've witnessed miracles. I've also been led into the darkest valley and challenged to the point of surrender. Sitting in that white room, however, I had no idea what was coming. I imagined it would all become easy. I figured Jesus would zap out the hard parts, cure my marriage problems and make everything okay. There would be one big bang and it would all be fixed. God, however, had different plans, and in many ways these last two years have been more painful than any other stretch of my adult life.

Still, even in my darkest times, I've had the blood of Jesus dripping into my veins - and there is no fluid on earth or in heaven more necessary for life.

Part Two:

Caitlyn

Delicate Chain

Caitlyn was still in rough shape - that dump truck had nearly killed her - but we had stopped the bleeding and filled her tank. We had now arrived at a critical moment: if her heart could start beating without help, she would have a chance. If it didn't, she would die.

I was still gripping her aorta in my fist when we removed the CPR machine. The room grew quiet and I focused on my fingertips, hoping to detect even the slightest flutter. In the terrible moment between life and death, I began to pray but was immediately interrupted by the thump of Caitlyn's heart - not only beating but pounding. I cried out to my team, "We've got a pulse here!"

It was great news, but we don't take time to celebrate in the OR, not when there is work to be done. We immediately turned our focus to the source of the blood loss: her pelvis and spleen. The pelvis had been packed but her spleen had to come out immediately. It was a simple procedure and we performed it without complications. After it had been removed, we closed her temporarily and attached a mechanism to her belly which was essentially a sponge attached to a vacuum.

Caitlyn had pulled through. Dead minutes before, she was now stable enough to leave the operating room for the Intensive Care Unit. Still, it was not yet time to relax. Her body had borne a terrible insult, and after such a trauma patients often spiral down a proverbial toilet. We need to stay vigilant and do our job in order to stop them before they pass the point of no return and flush out. With Caitlyn, we had to warm her up and replace clotting factors. We had to make sure she was clearing acid. She had little blood flow for over an hour so we had to check: Had her kidneys shut down? Is the bowel going into shock? Is her liver losing function? Even if the answer is 'no' to all these questions, there still could have been a serious injury to other parts of her body. There was a chance we had fixed the belly and filled the tank of someone with a non-survivable brain trauma.

All of these possibilities were on my mind as I made my way to the waiting room. Caitlyn was alive but she was still in so much danger I didn't know what to tell her family. As I walked, I prayed, asking Jesus to be present during our discussion.

Her father and grandmother were huddled together on the couch. They looked up at me - eyes wide, faces pale - clearly terrified. I had planned on calmly explaining the complicated medical situation, but something came over me and I blurted out, "She's alive!"

They cheered. They wept. They praised God. When it settled down, they looked at me and I showed them the cross.

A few minutes before, as I had left the operating room,

a nurse handed me a little clear cup and told me to give it to Caitlyn's family. It contained a cross on a delicate chain. I asked, "Where did you get that?"

The nurse shrugged. "We just took it off her."

I couldn't believe it. "She was rammed by a dump truck, went through a full trauma resuscitation, had everything cut from her body and 30 to 40 minutes of CPR - but that was still on her?"

"We just took it off a few minutes ago."

"Anesthesia put lines in her neck!"

She shrugged again. "They never removed it."

I didn't know quite what it meant but I knew it was amazing. Her grandmother was in tears when I gave it to her. "Oh my God," she cried. "That cross." There was a quiet reverence in her voice. "We had it made from wedding rings - Caitlyn's great-grandmother's and her great-great-grandmother's. We melted them down into a cross and added a diamond from her great-great-grandmother's engagement ring. Then we put the cross on my gold chain. We were going to give it to Caitlyn for graduation but she discovered our secret so I gave it to her on her birthday. She wasn't even supposed to have it yet. I can't believe it made it through all this."

It was a God-thing and we were grateful, but it was time to get down to the hard news. I explained what we had been doing. I told them about the CPR and her open belly. I said she still had a long way to go and there was a lot we didn't know. For a long moment after I finished speaking, there was a buzzing silence filled with fear.

But Caitlyn's grandmother shook it off. She was a small woman filled with a boisterous energy and she said, "She's alive, thank God." She smiled gratefully and repeated,

"Thank God she's alive."

I gripped their hands in mine before I left. It occurred to me as I did that my hands had recently gripped an artery to keep Caitlyn from losing more blood. Now they held on to those she loved as I offered a silent prayer for healing and peace.

Posturing

In the morning José and I went to see Caitlyn and were pleased to learn she'd had a great night. Her kidneys were working, and she was clearing acid; everything in the belly was looking good. All signs were positive with one exception: a CT scan had shown some bleeding on her brain. If the damage was bad enough, she would never wake up.

We gathered at her bedside for the examination. I pushed on her belly, to see if her bowel was swelling. If it was, she could pop open her vacuum closure. As I pressed down, she moved in a functional way.

I said to Jose, "Did you see that?"

"Yeah, I did."

"She just had a pain response."

José grinned and said, "This girl's going to be fine."

The ICU team wasn't as convinced. A pain response can be a sign of higher function, but some patients with complex brain injuries do predictable movements when they are touched. It's called posturing, and it can be a reflex, not a sign of brain activity. The team started to explain the CT findings, but José remained confident.

"No, she's with us," he said. "She's in there."

With no real evidence except for a gut feeling, I agreed. Caitlyn was still with us. She was going to be healed.

The next day one of my partners took her to the operating room. The pelvic packing came out without problem and the belly looked pristine. Nothing was swollen, she didn't have shock bowel, her liver wasn't damaged, and there were no other injuries. Once again, I was amazed. This young woman barely had a pulse for two hours the day before, but now she was looking great.

It was nothing short of a miracle - except for the brain injury. After they closed her, they had dropped sedation but Caitlyn wasn't waking up. There was nothing else to do but wait.

Days went by. Caitlyn's family kept vigil beside her bed, but they saw no sign of improvement. One morning I came to visit and her grandmother was there. The mood was grim. Clearly close to despair, she asked me if Caitlyn would ever wake up.

I offered professional platitudes. I assured her that these things take time, but I was losing faith myself. Silently, I agonized over the grandmother's grief. What if José and I had been wrong? Had we fixed the body of a girl who was already gone?

I checked her closures and found her anatomy was healing well. Then, when I pressed down on her abdomen, she moved.

I asked her grandmother, "Did you see that?"

A cautious smile appeared on her face.

I leaned close to Caitlyn's ear and yelled her name but received no response. "Caitlyn," I cried out again. "Open your eyes!"

Her head moved, a finger fluttered, and she gave a low moan. Behind me, her grandmother shouted with joy.

Again, I loudly called out her name, and again she groaned. But this time she turned her head slightly towards the sound, and then - for the first time in almost a week - she opened her eyes.

Her grandmother shoved me aside. "Caitlyn!" she shouted. She clutched at her granddaughter's hand. "You're fine. You've been in an accident, but you're fine."

Caitlyn tried to move and when she couldn't, she looked down at her body. To help her bones heal properly, the orthopedic team had attached a support system to her pelvis which sticks straight up from her hips. "Grandma," she mumbled, "they've turned me into a boy."

"That's Caitlyn!" Her grandmother laughed. "She's back!"

From there, Caitlyn flew through recovery. She was soon moved out of the ICU to our trauma floor and then healed so well they decided to bypass the rehab unit and discharge her straight to her home. When I saw her the day before she left, she was beat up but smiling. She seemed to glow.

Ten days later she rolled her wheelchair across the stage at graduation. Under her robe she wore a T-shirt which read, "I'm tougher than a dump-truck."

The Bucket

We often see God as our personal bucket of water. We like to think we can tuck him away somewhere and bring him out only in case of fire. Billy Graham talks about this in his book, This Is Why I Believe. He writes about how much safer it feels to believe we can keep God contained. As long as we know how deep our bucket goes and how wide it is, then he can't surprise us. We don't have to worry about being challenged. And we always know where he is in case of an emergency.

There are times, however, when this way of thinking becomes impossible, and God explodes out from our proverbial buckets. For me, this is what happened with Caitlyn. If you simply look at the data, the conclusion cannot be ignored. She was clinically dead for well over an hour. The action we took shouldn't have been successful. She had been too far gone to save. Yet she lived.

Many people - desperate to keep God safely contained in their buckets - try to explain it away. "She was young," they say, "and had a lot in reserve." While this is true, it resolves only 90% of how she was healed. It doesn't get us all the way there. We cannot bridge that gap without the Impossible Healer being involved.

No, what happened to Caitlyn was a miracle. It was God calling out from the middle of her story: "I'm here. I'm with you guys. This is me." Ultimately, it was evidence of a Healer who was bigger than a surgeon, bigger than our trauma system, bigger than all of us. God was out of the bucket.

It was not long after this, on a warm cloudless evening at the end of spring, that God offered me a glimpse of just how big He is. I stepped onto my back deck after a long shift. My knees cracked as I sat on a bench and looked up at the sky. There was a tugging sensation deep within me. I was new to faith, but knew enough to close my eyes and listen. I felt different: filled up with light. The fearful, buzzing silence - which had been pestering me most of my adult life - had been transformed into the thunderous silence of the presence of God.

When I thought of God that night, I pictured a body of water so large it disappeared into the horizon. It swelled and crashed along the shore. I dipped my toe and found it to be warm. I waded in, then dove, swimming down past the sea turtles but I couldn't tell how deep it was. I kept going until the surface faded above and it was all water around me in every direction. It was only a picture in my mind, a glimpse, but for the first time I understood in my limited way that God is bigger than I had ever imagined. In that place of prayer I floated up, bobbing gently up and down with the waves.

I felt a tugging, almost an itch. I was close to something true. I had pictured the ocean, but God was even bigger.

But what was bigger than the ocean?

I lost the moment. Whatever I was supposed to understand I had missed. In frustration, I lay my head back against the chair and opened my eyes. There the night sky was spread before me. The stars shone with a brilliance I had never seen before. It was an explosion of size and space and wonder. And it was as if God spoke directly into my heart, saying, "Tom, I'm even bigger."

My bucket had overturned. God was on the loose. He was bigger than anything I could ever have imagined - and he was doing the impossible.

Fruitcake

To be honest, none of this has been easy for me to acknowledge. It can be difficult for any surgeon or scientist to credit the Impossible Healer. Part of it is our own ego. When things go right, we want the fingers pointing toward us. We want everyone to know how skilled we are; how gifted and brilliant. We don't want some God to distract people from worshipping us. So it is difficult to talk about God in the hospital partly because of ego - but also because of Moses.

Moses was an unlikely choice to lead the Israelites out of Egypt. He was an outsider; he grew up around Egyptian royalty and not among the Hebrew slaves. He couldn't speak properly; the Bible says he had a speech impediment. Worst of all, he was a murderer; he killed an Egyptian guard in anger after witnessing the man's abuse. Still, God said, "You're doing it. I got this boy, Aaron, and he'll speak for you. Trust me. I've got you."

After they made a fool out of Pharaoh first with the plagues and then by crossing the Red Sea, the Hebrew slaves escaped Egypt[1] and fled into the wilderness. There, Moses climbed up the mountain to meet with God.[2] The next stage of the journey was uncertain and Moses wanted to ensure that God would continue to lead them. "If you are not going along, do not send us," Moses said. "Show me you're with us. Show me your glory."

"Listen," God said, "if I show up in all my glory, you'll die. My greatness would melt you."

I think most of us would bow out right there, but Moses was greedy for God. He begged the Almighty, "Just give me a little something, even a nubbin."

God relented. "Okay, I'll stick you on a rock and cover you up with my hand. When I pass by I'll move my hand and you can look."

In medicine, we use a particular formula based on body surface area to calculate burn percentage. If God was covered by a robe and if he exposed the skin of one calf as he walked away from Moses, then by this formula Moses saw roughly 1% of God. It was only a sliver, but it was enough to make the man glow.

While Moses was gone, the Israelites had dug the idols out of storage. It would become a familiar pattern. God does an amazing thing; the people quickly forget; and at the first opportunity they turn away. Here, God had rescued them from four hundred years of slavery. He gave them a sound and light show with pillars of cloud and fire. He parted the sea. Still, the first time they were left on their own, they wanted to party it up. They looked to Aaron who said, "Hey, are they gone? Let's bring out the calf!"

Later, when Moses came down from the mountain

---

1   You should look it up in Exodus 1-12. It's a great story.

2   Exodus 33

and caught them worshipping a hunk of gold, they were not at all ashamed. Instead, they thought Moses was nuts. They cried out, "What's wrong with that guy? He's glowing. What a fruitcake! Get him out of here!" They forced him to cover his face with a veil. The people didn't want a living reminder of the God who rescued them - in this case it was Moses - to distract them from their lifeless hunks of gold.

In a similar way, it can be risky to bring God into the hospital. Those who talk about the Impossible Healer - about a God loosed from the bucket - are often seen as being fruitcakes. Many even consider them a danger to the scientific process.

Like in ancient Israel, we keep getting this backwards. We call the light darkness and the darkness light. In a thousand subtle ways, the message is, "Hey Blee, we've got a guy here who jumped out of a second floor building. He is covered with blood but he doesn't have any injuries because as it turns out it isn't his blood. He had butchered someone upstairs. Could you talk to him? But don't go crazy and bring up faith. Don't mention that nutty Jesus stuff. Just talk to him about jumping out of a building while covered in someone else's blood."

We are surrounded by deeply injured people longing for healing, but for some in the medical field healing is the last thing they want us to discuss. Underneath the chatter, this is what I hear, "Hey Blee, we got this guy out of the ICU. He's barfed up seventeen bags of cocaine. We know he's a big dealer. Can you talk to him? Don't talk to him about some impossible healing because that's crazy. Stick to barfing up cocaine."

I see it every day. I'll encounter a young woman with pus oozing from an abscess in her elbow - a result from injecting meth or ground up oxycontin. It's rotting her arm out, but this is considered normal. No matter how dark and hurtful it may be, people are comfortable with it. Yet any discussion about God and the path to true healing is outside the bounds, even considered dangerous.

It comes down to this: All of us at times prefer to create and worship our own golden calves. Our idols - though ultimately destructive - are safe and predictable while the Impossible Healer is out of our control. In the hospital, idols comes in the form of such things as the false adoration from our patients and their families, treatments used from only one study, or an unworkable solution suggested because it gives us the illusion of authority.

I am often as guilty of this as anyone. It is dangerous when God is out of the bucket and so I often refuse to see God even when he is right in front of me. Like the disciples did when Jesus walked across the water, I forget the many miracles I have witnessed and tell myself I am seeing something I'm not. I am as blind as anyone, which is why Caitlyn was so significant. I know God healed Caitlyn. It was a knock-me-on-my-knees, holy-cow, that-was-the-coolest-thing-I've-ever-seen miracle. My bucket had overturned, and no pathetic idol could compare to the impossible healing Jesus would bring.

Zap

The path to impossible healing is simple: Follow the Healer. That's it. It isn't complicated. You don't need a fancy degree. You don't need to study abstract philosophies. Keep your eyes on Jesus and keep walking.

It is simple, but when it came to my own struggles I didn't want simple. I wanted it to be easy. My marriage had been in trouble for years and it was approaching the end; I wanted God to raise it from the dead. "We need a miracle, Jesus," I'd pray. "Zap us." I wanted the hard parts to be taken away, and God could have done that, but he had bigger plans. I wanted the quick fix, but he was leading me down the path to impossible healing.

Greg Laurie, pastor of Harvest Christian Fellowship in Riverside California, offers this example: You have been hired to do a job, and your employer has given you two pay options. You can get paid $25,000 on the first of the month, or they'll pay you a penny today, two pennies tomorrow, four pennies the next day, then eight, then sixteen, and so on. Which would you choose?

Me, I'd want the twenty-five grand. I want the big bang - but Pastor Laurie points out that if we can be patient and wait; if we can take the small but escalating payments over time, then after thirty days we would have over five million dollars.

We want God to give us the easy solution, but he works in a completely different way. For me, I wanted my personal life fixed but instead God sent me on the most difficult journey I have ever been on. In the year after I got on my knees in the white room, it seemed every new day was worse than the one before. I prayed more times than I can count, "I can't do this any more. You aren't listening to a thing I say."

In my weakness I wanted to take the easier paths. I wanted to chase money, even though if we hang with God, he will fill our life with true treasure. I was tired and wanted to give up, even though if we hang with God, he will give us true rest. I wanted to scratch for little pleasures, even though if we hang with God he will show us true joy.

So I argued with God. I wanted healing on my timeline. I wanted my problems to go away. Instead I found myself walking the edge of the death canyon, feeling entirely alone. I wanted to quit but Jesus kept saying:

"Tom, hang with me. Keep it simple and seek out my face. Dark times, light times, no matter what I promise I'll be there.

"I don't work on the time that you guys work on. I always have been, and I always will be. I AM![1] I know you want healing and I love you so much you're going to get it, but it will be in my way.

"Watch for me in your life and in the people around

---

[1]   See Exodus 3:14

you and I will give glimmers of hope every day. I know it won't be easy, but I promise it will be simple - and simply amazing!"

Sure, I wanted the concrete moment. I didn't want a penny today and two pennies tomorrow - I wanted the big payoff now. But if God gave it to me now, I would miss out on something much bigger down the road, a healing so big it wouldn't fit in a book.

It's a common human weakness: we impatiently throw together solutions that appear cool at first but in reality they suck. If however we grunt it out and do what's simple - follow Jesus - God will make it glorious.

It is a simple path. Follow Jesus. No tricks or twists, just one foot in front of another. It has been a messy journey and a hard one, but it was leading towards impossible healing. The first thing I needed to learn was how to trust him. And to do that I needed to do something dangerous: I needed to pray.

Part Two:

Eric

Prayer Chain

One quiet summer day Eric went on a bike ride as he had several times a week for many years. He would often take long detours through the rolling hills around his small Wisconsin city so when he was late returning home, his wife at first thought nothing of it.

Hours later, however, she was in a full panic when she was finally contacted by the police. A woman had found Eric laying unconscious next to his bike. She had called for an ambulance and performed CPR until the sheriff department arrived. They raced him to the hospital but it was too late. He was alive, but essentially brain dead.

Eric was one of the doctors who trained me. He was a gifted physician, and everyone at the hospital loved him. He had a wonderful wife and three amazing kids. He reached out to his residents and welcomed us into his home. He taught us how to operate and how to care for people - but even more, he taught us how to live.

After hearing the news, I spent the next several hours on the phone with grieving colleagues around the country; men and women whose lives had been profoundly impacted by this man. Desperate to do something, I started a prayer chain through text messages, writing, "It's time to buckle down and ask God for healing."

I engaged people who didn't even know Eric: friends from LIFEteam, John Turnipseed,[1] and friends from church. It was a mixed group which made a bell-shaped curve: On one end were those who were extremely comfortable with prayer. In the middle were those who would shake their heads, not sure what to think. And in the far end were those who absolutely didn't believe. I myself was floating around the middle. It was all still new and I didn't feel solid on prayer yet - but I was trying to get better. This prayer chain was a step in that direction.

One man - a dear friend of Eric's - was on the far end of the curve. He messaged me separately, "Do you really think if we pray hard enough he's going to be okay?" He was struggling, grieving for his friend. He wrote, "He's in full blown brain death. He's having constant seizures. There's nothing that could help him now.

"Tom, listen," he wrote, "Eric is not going to heal."

---

1   You will learn about LIFEteam and John Turnipseed in Chapter Four.

Lazarus

I'm a surgeon and a scientist. I believe in looking at the data. I believe in studying the facts, and the fact is that good people die all the time.

This creates a conflict because we know God can heal any situation - no matter how impossible. As Caitlyn's surgeon, I witnessed this first hand, but God has been doing it since the beginning.

In his gospel, John writes about a man named Lazarus[1] who was one of Jesus' closest friends. Lazarus becomes sick while Jesus is off in another city. When Jesus finally arrives in Bethany where Lazarus was living, he finds the man's sisters, Mary and Martha, weeping. They crumple in front of him, wailing over their brother who had died in Jesus' absence.

The Bible says that Jesus wept with them. When he saw their heartache, he joined them in their grief. Then he went to the tomb where Lazarus lay, the stink of death pouring from it, and he cried out, "Lazarus, get out of there!" And

---

[1]   John 11:1-44

it was a miracle, a moment of impossible healing: Lazarus stood; he was bound by funeral cloths, but alive.

In this story I hear again Jesus saying, "I've got you." Even when all seemed lost, Jesus had Lazarus in his arms. He had been dead for days but Jesus brought him back to life.

Jesus is the Impossible Healer. If he can raise a man from the dead, he could certainly heal my friend. But here is the hard part: people who are being prayed for just as hard as we prayed for Eric often don't get any better.

This past spring we had a young woman[2] in our trauma bay with a brain injury. Earlier in the day, she was riding in a car which made a soft left into her friend's driveway. In a hurry, she unfastened her seatbelt and opened her passenger door, anticipating by seconds when the car would make a complete stop. But it jostled wrong and she spilled out, slamming her head against the pavement. They rushed her to us but it was immediately clear she had a non-survivable brain trauma. There was nothing we could do, and so, at three o'clock in the morning, it was my job to sit down with her family.

They received the news silently, in shock. As I brought them back to the surgical ICU, the injured woman's brother couldn't walk; he kept doubling over, collapsing under the weight of his grief. His parents were praying desperately. All I could do was put my arm around the father and be present as he wept. I wanted for this kid what Caitlyn had received. I prayed for healing, whatever it would be in that situation. I prayed for peace. I prayed for a miracle.

Two days later, the young woman died.

It creates a painful tension: I believe in healing and

---

2   Essential details of this person's story have been changed.

prayer, but I am a surgeon who encounters death every day. I know healing doesn't often happen like it did for Lazarus or Caitlyn. I know that Eric's friend was probably right, and Eric would not be healed - but that didn't stop me from asking God for it. I wanted the Lazarus moment. I wanted the zap. I wanted the miracle.

Around the country - even the world - people were pleading with God that Eric might be healed, but he only grew worse. Finally, a few days after the accident, the doctors had to remove life support. Still we kept praying but it wasn't long before Eric died.

It was a hard time. Saying goodbye to a good friend always hurts, so there was grief, but I also struggled with the real possibility that Eric's friend was right on the larger point. Maybe there was no such thing as impossible healing.

The Funeral

The funeral was so large Eric's family had to rent out a convention center. Many stood up to speak about him and they each did a beautiful job. He was a man who had lived a good, Godly life, and both joy and gratitude were expressed in the midst of their grief. It was already a powerful service, but when it was almost over Eric's wife stepped to the microphone. In a voice both clear and calm, she offered words of grace. She thanked everyone for coming. She thanked the speakers for their kind and honest words. Then she said, "These last days have been the worst in my life, but I am grateful. I am grateful I had time with my husband to say goodbye. I am grateful we had time with friends and family. And then I'm grateful that - in the middle of all of it - something remarkable happened."

She told us a story about a young girl who experienced a trauma a couple of years earlier. Some of the details were lost to me, but this is what I heard: The sheriff had assisted at the scene before they raced her off in the ambulance. At the hospital, Eric was involved in her care and they did what they could, but it was too late, and the girl died. She was eight years old.

When Eric had his heart attack, the woman who found him and performed CPR was the mother of the little girl. The first on the scene for Eric was the same sheriff who raced to care for the little girl. In the last days of his life, around his hospital bed, a grieving mother, a sheriff and Eric's wife talked and wept. Tragedy had brought them together.

She finished her story by saying, "In the middle of this nightmare, it was a time of amazing healing."

The Cave

As a scientist I struggle with this, but it's true: at the heart of impossible healing is something we cannot measure. It is almost beyond description, except John points us to it when he writes, 'The light shines in the darkness, and the darkness has not overcome it.'[1]

Impossible healing is light in the middle of a deep darkness. It is light when all feels lost, when it looks like your loved one will never recover. It is light even in the heart of the death canyon, where you cannot see your next step.

A few years back I took my sons to a cave a couple hours drive from our home. There, they took us hundreds of feet below the surface of the earth and at one point they shut off all the lights. It was painful; my senses hurt. The guide lowered her voice an octave and told us that it only took a few minutes really, less than a half an hour, for your eyes to be affected by the darkness. They change; their rods and cones which are built to receive light began to degrade. If you were to stay in that darkness - the guide continued

---

1   John 1:5

ominously - for no more than a few hours, you could lose your sight permanently. The darkness would quickly overwhelm you... forever.

This guide was a showman and not a medical professional so feel free to shut off all your lights when you go to bed tonight. Still, it is true that darkness has a powerful effect on our world. When you are in a place of utter despair it does not take long before your senses begin to numb, before your brain begins to misfire, before you want to give up. You cannot find the light and - buried there - you begin to believe the darkness has won forever.

There in the pit, you have no options left. There is nothing you can do but cling to an impossible hope and trust the One who can bring the light; the One who shines in the darkness.

Impossible healing is God showing up in ways we cannot possibly orchestrate. It is God shining into places so dark we cannot believe light even exists anymore. Sometimes it looks like a miracle that blows our minds. Sometimes it looks like a ripple in a pond, smaller moments which reach out and touch everyone it encounters. Sometimes it is simply hope in Jesus' promise, "I've got you," even when the world is collapsing around us.

Return to Lazarus

It can be hard to trust this promise, particularly in the face of death, but in the end healing is guaranteed. Jesus promises us eternal life - a place in heaven where there is no pain; there are no tears. When we get there, we're going to fly. Ultimately our friend Eric died but we continue to trust that he will be healed. Raised in Christ, his brain trauma, the seizures, they will all be gone. God might not have fixed him in the hospital, but he healed him for eternity. And all that prayer? We may not have even known it ourselves, but we were praying for healing that touched everyone involved in remarkable ways.

After the funeral I revisited the Lazarus story in John 11 and I found it didn't quite go as I had remembered. Martha and Mary had sat at Jesus' feet and listened to his words. Their brother was a dear friend of his. They believed in him - and they expected a miracle. When Lazarus became sick, even as he reached the edge of death, they were confident Jesus would show up and make their brother well. But Jesus was delayed, so they sent a message. Another day passed. Jesus still didn't show up. Finally, Lazarus died.

At this point Mary and Martha might still have expected Jesus - he had raised Jairus' daughter from the dead after all - but the next day Lazarus was wrapped in grave clothes and his body laid into the tomb. Three more days passed and no Jesus - no miracle - no zap.

Four days after Lazarus died Jesus finally arrived in Bethany, and Martha and Mary both cried out, "Where were you? We were waiting for your healing but you didn't show up."

Jesus showed no frustration with their impatience, but instead he cried with them. Then, after sharing in their grief, he stood at the edge of the tomb and cried out for Lazarus to get out of there - and the man who had been dead for four days was raised back to life.

At the end of this story I came across a key sentence: "Therefore many of the Jews who had come to visit Mary, and had seen what Jesus did, believed in him."[1] Healing came for Lazarus. It wasn't as Mary and Martha expected, but because of the way Jesus did it, people all around were healed. He gathered a crowd of naysayers and knocked them all down with a miracle. This wouldn't have happened if Jesus had simply snapped his fingers from the beginning.

When God gets involved healing moves beyond what we could orchestrate. It can be surprising, even weird. He says, "Your sick family member will be healed, I guarantee it. She might have to die first, but no matter what, I've got her. And I promise no more tears, no more pain, no more grief." The ultimate healing may have to wait until eternity but still God gives us these surprises, these ripples of healing that touch everyone near. Maybe through a trauma

---

1   John 11:45

God will heal a family member in the midst of her grief. Or a nurse suffering heartache from an ongoing battle at home will reengage life in a new way. The healing in these lives will ripple out, touching dozens passing through families and communities until hundreds are made more whole. Impossible healing may not be on our timeline and it might not be the sound and light show we expect, but it will often expand out into something bigger - and more glorious - than we would ever have imagined.

Part Four:

Keyonte

Soul of the Belly

Several years ago Keyonte - who everyone called Tay - had a kid from the neighborhood giving him a hard time. The kid drew a knife and stabbed Tay hard enough to send him to the hospital. It was a serious but not life threatening wound and Tay was soon released. The other kid moved away and for a long time life in the neighborhood was relatively quiet until, a few days before I met him, Tay ran into that same kid in a grocery store.

Tay confronted him but the kid denied the stabbing - swore that Tay had the wrong guy - but words turned to shoving and shoving turned to fighting. They moved from the store and into the parking lot. There, the kid reached into a pocket and Tay heard the sound of a firecracker. The kid ran away and Tay started walking home. He made it a block before he realized he couldn't move his hand. It took him a moment more to realize he had been shot.

The bullet struck Tay in the upper right quadrant of his belly, an area we call the soul of the abdomen. It is filled with complex anatomy, including the pancreas and huge blood vessels. It is among the most dangerous places to be injured.

He was brought into the trauma center with his bowel hanging out. As one of my partners unzipped him in the operating room he could actually hear blood whooshing from the wound. Then the surgeon did what needed to be done. He stuck fingers where necessary to stop bleeding, and he fired stitches. When he was done and Tay was stable, they vacuumed packed the wound and sent him to the ICU.

The team expected Tay to come back for more repairs after he had some time to straighten out on his own - but there was something seriously wrong: He was still producing acid; he wasn't making urine. They checked under his temporary closure and found his bowel was dusky. They ran him through testing: a CT scan and a roadmap of his blood vessels. From this they discovered the bullet had hit a major artery in the soul of his abdomen. His small intestine, which was downstream from the wound, wasn't getting enough blood.

Tay went back to the operating room with the original trauma surgeon and two of our vascular surgeons. They didn't have many options but these are men and women who are excellent at their jobs. They took some veins out of his legs and used them to fire in a couple of jump grafts. The hope was this would offer a temporary bypass around the wound so blood could flow where it was needed. It worked, but only to a point. His bowels were kept alive, but barely.

It was the last days of May, 2014. I had been away during all of Tay's treatment to this point, but as I started my shift a colleague reported, "There's a kid upstairs who's had several operations and an open abdomen. They took out some bowel and left him in discontinuity. You'll need to hook him back up and close him."

I'm a general surgeon, which means I can open a skull, reset a bone, or sew up a bullet hole in the heart, but we typically bring in special teams to do much of that work. General surgeons typically direct traffic, but we specialize in the belly. I knew almost nothing about him at this point, but Tay had a belly wound so I became his physician. He was a skinny kid, eighteen years old at most, and his anatomy was easy; I hooked him up, closed him, and put him in the intensive care unit. I didn't think much about him after that but went on to the next patient.

A couple days later he came back to my trauma floor with an abdomen needing bowel function. Every time we tried to feed him his intestines screamed back at us, "It's not going to work!" He bloated up like a toad and vomited all over the place. He had profuse diarrhea - or so we thought at first. We quickly figured out it wasn't food matter coming through him; he didn't have enough blood supply for that. No, he was actually sloughing his intestinal lining. He was in a lot of trouble and a lot of pain.

His pain was more than physical. The atmosphere in his room was heavy. He was awake and alert but would not engage with me, refusing to speak a single word. He pulled the bedsheets to his nose. With the lights off and the blinds pulled, it was always dark, even in the middle of the afternoon.

Still, we did what we could. We shut down all of his food intake and put in an IV. Feeding him by vein would give his intestines enough of a break, we reasoned, to give his body time to build more blood vessels. But the process would take weeks, so when he was stable enough we gave his mother instruction on how to use the IV and sent him home.

Five days later Tay was back in the hospital. His IV had become infected. He had bacteria all through his blood. He was just about dead and again ended up in the intensive care unit. We did a heart ultrasound and found two heart valves were being chewed up by bacteria. The veins in his chest and arms were clotted up from the feeding line. They had to put an IV in his foot because it was the only part of his body that would work.

After four days, they had brought him through the infection and he ended back upstairs with me. He was stable but still broken, still beaten down, still looking terrible. In my previous life, before getting on my knees in the white room, I probably would have walked in, felt a twisting discomfort that we couldn't fix him, and walked out. Maybe I would have splashed a little water from my God-bucket and prayed limply, "Jesus - this kid's got trouble."

I wasn't that person any more. Instead, I remembered Jesus' words to crazy Peter in the water. "I've got you," he said. I knew if it was a promise for me then Jesus was holding on to Tay as well. The thought kept tugging me back into his darkened room. I wanted to see a flicker of hope inside the kid with the belly wound.

I sat near his bed. His eyes were open but he did not look at me. I spoke plainly. "Tay, we have a problem. We can't feed you because your guts don't work. And we don't have a vein source because your body's clotted everything off. On top of all that, your heart's being chewed up by infection. So we are out of options. We're going to keep working medically, but honestly... you need a miracle.

And if it's okay I'd like to introduce you to the only miracle I know. His name is John Turnipseed."

Turnipseed

In the weeks after I fell on my knees in the white room Jesus kept showing up all around me. Boom - he spoke through a radio lecture during my commute. Boom - he spoke through a book I was reading. Boom - he spoke through a moment of impossible healing in the trauma bay. Wherever I looked, he was there.

Unsurprisingly, I encountered Jesus at church as well. The Sunday after the white room, I joined my sister for worship at River Valley Church led by Rob Ketterling. He was going through a series called Dangerous Prayers. As he spoke I felt a burning conviction grow in my chest. That night I began to pray those prayers before I went to bed. "Not my will, but yours be done," I would pray, and "I'm here, God. I'm listening. Let me have it."

A couple of weeks passed, and I assimilated the data from the lectures, the books, the daily miracles, and Pastor Ketterling's message as best I could. Through them, God brought me to a place where I was ready to say, "The data makes sense and I'm ready to go all in. Jesus, let me see what you're going to do."

I started listening and watching. I kept saying those prayers. Within a week, two young men from two different gangs were both brought to our hospital. They had both been shot. After their wounds were patched up, they were placed on our trauma floor in rooms next door to each other. The ensuing chaos of the situation shut down the hallway.

It was April which was too early in the year for this kind of event. One of our veteran nurses understood how things were supposed to work and said to me, "This is all wrong; it isn't trauma season yet." She pointed a finger at my chest. "You need to fix this."

I asked, "Why are you pointing at me?"

She glared sternly and said, "Because you're standing here."

Her words echoed another dangerous prayer, this one from Isaiah: Here I am, send me.[1] There was a thundering silence after she walked away, and I said to God, "If this is one of the things you're throwing at me, I'm listening. Let's do this."

With equal parts terror and excitement, I approached one of the families filling the hallway. I tried to get their attention, tried to find a way into the chaos, but they were too worked up to pay much notice. Unfazed, I pushed my way into the next room, but, if possible, they ignored me even more. This being the first time I followed a prompting of the Spirit, it was confusing. I had expected a bigger pay off. Still, the chaos began to settle down on its own, and for that I was thankful.

Two days passed without any further incident, and I

---

1   Isaiah 6:8

began to doubt my calling. Maybe I had misunderstood. Maybe the nurse was just venting her frustration and I happened to be standing nearby. At that time I was running to shame before confidence. I was running to fear before I ran to Jesus. So - as was my habit - I put the blame on myself: I was too weak and wounded. My personal life was a mess and I had all this crud inside me. I thought I was ready to go all in, but it didn't matter. There was no way God would want any help from a guy like me. Still, I kept saying these dangerous prayers. I kept crying out, "Here am I, Jesus. Use me." I didn't know what else to say; I had no fancy words to add. "Use me, Lord," I'd pray again and again. "Use me."

My sister called the next day. "There is a guy on the radio you need to work with," she said. "His name is Mr. Turnipseed. Twenty years ago he was Minnesota's worst gang-banger. He'd been shot ten times. He has thirty family members in prison. He was a drug dealer and a pimp but he's free from all that now. His former gang territory went from being called 'Crack Alley' to being a nationally recognized program named Urban Ventures."

The interview was from Real Recovery Radio on the local Christian station. It was late when I got home but I found it online and listened straight through until it was after midnight. When the program ended, the house around me was perfectly still and the thunder from the silence rolled over me. Something was happening - something big. I searched for John Turnipseed online and learned he was writing a book with a company called Five Stone Media. It was led by a man named Steve Johnson.

I was too worked up to wait until morning so I sent a message to Steve in the middle of the night. It read, "I'm a trauma surgeon in Saint Paul. These kids keep shooting each other in this revolving door of violence. They come in, we fix them up and they go shoot someone else. We pull them out of the fire but we can't bring them to the light. Do you think John could help?"

Steve's answer came the next morning. His message simply read, "John's all in. Let's have lunch."

He directed me to a restaurant towards inner city Minneapolis. At noon the next day I pulled into the parking lot. A sign there read, "Minneapolis police advises locking your valuables in the trunk of your car." I started getting nervous. I was meeting with a gangster in a sketchy part of town. What was I doing there? I almost turned around - but my fear vanished when John Turnipseed arrived. He greeted me warmly and shook my hand. He wore a suit and tie which made me feel dingy in comparison but it didn't matter. There was something about him that was instantly comforting.

The life experiences which brought us to that lunch couldn't have been more different - but we hit it off immediately. After a lunch filled with laughter and stories, I told him about the situation at the hospital. He listened carefully then said, "Listen Tom, there's no kid we can't get out of a gang. When they start doing things right, the gangs get bored. When we start wrapping our arms around them, the gangs get bored. And if we get to the point where we can't get the kid out of the gang I will walk up to the leaders and tell them, 'This one is mine. I've got him. Let him go.'"

His words whacked me. It was the first time I had heard that piercing, "I've got you," since reading about Jesus reaching down to save Peter from the water. After we said our good-byes, there was thunder in the silence of the car as I drove away. I had prayed those dangerous prayers and something was really happening: God wasn't messing around. He had orchestrated a new friendship between two very different men, and - as we met and talked and dreamed over the next several weeks - our friendship led to a movement we would call LIFEteam.

The hospital has two teams for end of life: hospice and palliative care, and we wanted a team focused on helping people through the other parts of life. LIFE stands for Leadership Impacting the Family Environment - and the idea behind it is simple. As medical professionals we need to do the things we do well. In the trauma center, we are experts at patching people up - this is our strike zone and we shouldn't stray too far from it. But after the physical body has been fixed, we need to bring outside resources into the hospital to lead the patient into the next part of healing. Together we can help them deal with housing, criminal stuff, gangs, drugs - or whatever else they are facing. Once the program got moving, we were able to find a solution to any problem the client threw at us.

We quickly learned that a hospital is the ideal setting for LIFEteam. It is only after most people have lost everything and have stared death in the eyes that they are ready for impossible healing.

Two Guys Talking

John Turnipseed and I had spent several weeks putting together a program which we hoped would bring real healing - the impossible kind - into the lives of the kids coming through the trauma bay. God had brought together an unlikely team: A trauma surgeon[1], a former gangbanger turned minister[2], the CEO of Urban Ventures[3], and the head of Five Stone Media[4]. It was clear He was up to something big, and we could feel it. In a fit of inspiration I spent one afternoon setting goals, dreaming through the next month, three months, and year. At the two year mark I wrote, 'We will start a foundation and spread LIFEteam to communities all around the nation.'

We were ready. We were all in, but before any part of the vision could be realized, we had to take our first tentative steps. In late May, I saw our first opportunity to put the idea to work: Tay, the kid with the belly wound.

1   Me.
2   John Turnipseed.
3   At the time, it was Tim Clark.
4   Steve Johnson.

I sat next to him on his hospital bed. His room was dark. His sheets were pulled up past his chin. His eyes were cold and sullen. The process had yet to be refined, but the kid needed a miracle and I knew John could help. Here was the moment for which God had been preparing us.

"Tay," I said, "You need a miracle. I'd like to bring in a minister named John Turnipseed. I think he can help."

He muttered an answer. I couldn't understand him so I leaned in closer. I asked again, "Can I bring in John?"

This time he spoke the word clear enough for me to hear. "No."

It took me a moment to understand, and when I did there was a part of me which wanted to argue, but I didn't push. It was disappointing, but it was entirely his decision. After finishing my medical examination, I excused myself to tend to other patients.

An hour later I received a phone call from one of the nurses. "Tay's mom is up here demanding to talk to you. She wants to know why you told her son he's going to be dead."

Even as I thought, "I never said that," I knew I wasn't being entirely honest. It may not have been in those words exactly, but Tay had heard what I had meant. I hurried back to his floor, nervous his mom was going to yell at me, but when I entered the room it was clear she wasn't angry. She only wanted to hear for herself what I had told Tay.

I explained again, "Your son's intestines don't work so he can't eat - and we don't have a vein source for an IV because his body has clotted everything off."

She listened intently then asked, "What are we going to do?"

"He needs a miracle. I think he should talk to my

friend, John Turnipseed."

"Absolutely yes!" she said. "Let's bring him in."

From his bed, Tay again muttered, "No."

His mom's eyes flashed with anger. "Oh yes," she said, her voice stern. "You are going to talk to this man."

The mother had spoken and John came to visit the next day. He kept it low key - just two guys chatting. He asked some questions about what Tay wanted to do with his life, but mostly they simply spent time getting to know each other. The next afternoon, John came back. Then again the day after that.

Outside looking in, it was difficult to see the mechanism of it, but it was clear healing was taking place. When I visited later, Tay's bedsheets had lowered from his chin to his chest. It wasn't long before the lights in the room were turned on and Tay was sitting up. He began engaging with me when I visited, starting conversations with a smile. Barely a week had passed and sunlight and laughter filled the room. All from a little engagement with John Turnipseed.

During this time, Tay's body was healing as well. Ten days after his arrival, he had improved enough to eat. We were able to start a new IV line since he needed to take nutrition by vein at night. Soon he was strong enough to recover at home.

Two weeks later, John called me. "I just had dinner with Tay." He laughed happily. "He's doing great!"

I wasn't sure if I understood him. "Did you just say you had dinner with Tay?"

"Yep."

"Did you feed him?"

"Wasn't I supposed to?"

The last time I saw Tay, he had no working bowel. There were certain foods he could eat - he always wanted ice cream - but anything else would make him sick. "Did he sprint to the bathroom?"

"Nah, he was feeling good."

I couldn't believe this. I asked, "What did he eat?"

"A couple pieces of chicken, and I don't know. All kinds of stuff."

"Seriously?"

"Yeah."

"But he's all right?"

"He's fine."

Tay saw me for a routine followup a month later. He had survived a bullet wound. He had survived an infection which had chewed through his whole body. He had survived bacteria eating at the valves in his heart. Physically, he had taken about as bad a beating as the world could dish out, but when he came to see me he was beaming. His heart was repaired, the echo looked great. He was eating. His eyes were open. He was smiling. He was gaining weight. One of the last notes in his chart was written in capital letters: YOU ARE CURED.

John continued to work with him through LIFEteam, and it became a story of impossible healing; not only of the body but of the whole person. Tay still struggles but he's doing well. He's on a good path and has great support. He should have been dead, but instead he was where it started. Tay showed us LIFEteam would work.

God Sighs

I had done the simple thing. I spoke dangerous prayers and followed when I heard God call. It hadn't been easy, but through the experience, I witnessed the Impossible Healer transform a young man's life. I saw how Tay glowed; it had been simply amazing and I wanted it for myself.

But I was growing impatient: healing wasn't coming quickly enough. Finally, late one cloudless Friday night, I sat anguishing alone on my back deck. My personal life remained a hot mess - the weight of my many mistakes pressed down too heavily on my shoulders - and my new faith in Jesus hadn't been much help.

Desperate, I decided to call John Turnipseed. I had heard a little of his story with drugs and gangs but I assumed he had grown to a place where he no longer made mistakes. I had placed him high on a pedestal - he was a man who had it all figured out. After seeing him work with Tay I hoped he would be able to fix me as well. Second to Jesus, I was hoping John could save me.

When he answered the phone, I blurted out, "Can I talk

to you about my marriage?"

"Absolutely!" he said. "But…" he chuckled sadly and his voice grew soft, "you do know I've been married five times."

Later I would read his book, Bloodline, and learn how wrong I had been, but in that moment I was shocked. "What? I thought you had the one happy marriage."

He assured me that was not the case and began to share some of his story. We talked into the night. I discovered that this man I had revered as a saint had actually been a huge sinner. He told me both of the injuries he had suffered and the impossible healing he had received.

It was a surprising comfort to learn John Turnipseed was as broken as I was, and in the silence of the night after our conversation I again heard God thunder, "You think your pain runs deeper than others'? You think you know shame? Talk to Turnipseed. You don't think I can heal you? Listen to John. I healed him, and next to that, you're a chip shot." It was as crystal clear a message as I've ever heard.

In Mark 7, Jesus is healing a man who cannot speak. He pulls the man aside, looks up and sighs. Then Jesus licks his fingers, puts them in the man's ears and says, "Speak. You're healed. Ephatha," which means, "Be opened."

In his book, God Came Near, Max Lucado reflects on this story. He believes Christ sighs because the world shouldn't be this way. There shouldn't be sickness. There shouldn't be sin. The man Jesus was healing wasn't made to be mute. We weren't supposed to be broken. God made us whole and healthy, to walk with our heavenly Father in a place where suffering and death do not exist. Grief is at the heart of Jesus' sigh. Yet in the midst of his grief he heals the man - because healing is at the heart of Christ.

Lucado then writes about the time God spent with Adam and Eve. The Bible doesn't tell us how many years - maybe thousands - but for awhile everything was going great. The world was blissfully chugging away. Everyone was happy, living in perfect communion with each other. Eden was a wonderland until God walked around the corner to find Adam and Eve with fruit juice staining their chins. Eyes wide open to their own nakedness, they covered themselves as they wept. With a gut-wrenching sigh, God said, "Oh no! What did you do?"

What they had done was listen to the snake. They were given freedom to choose and they chose to eat the fruit. Jesus' sigh in Mark 7 can be traced back to that moment. The world simply wasn't the way it was meant to be.

But sin is also not the end of the story. Even as God grieves over Adam and Eve, he causes a new tree to grow behind them. Faced with our rebellion, he immediately starts to fix it, saying in essence, "I have a tree growing which will be made into a cross. My kid will hang on that tree and he will take all of this back." This is the power of that sigh. It is God loving us so much we stop him in his tracks. It is God promising he will do anything to rescue us.

Yet we continue to sin! There is the old saying: An apple a day keeps the doctor away. There is an irony there because it was an apple which kept the ultimate Healer away. It was fruit which caused that division, and we keep eating it to this day.

I see it in my own life. I see it in Turnipseed. In the trauma bay many of the apples are easy to spot: chronic alcoholism, drug abuse and other high risk behaviors. But we all have them and many are more subtle: tobacco or overeating, laziness or working too hard, neglecting our families or refusing to set good boundaries. Whatever it is for you, that apple you're eating is keeping the Healer away. These apples, these things we put in the place of God, every day they make Jesus sigh.

Some of the brokenness I encounter is so messed up, their apples are so huge and consuming that all I can do is point them to the new tree of life growing behind them. Only there at the cross will they find the healing they need. In the middle of the night, on the phone on my back porch, this is what John did for me.

My personal life never did get the zap I had wanted from God. Turnipseed wasn't dropped into my world to fix my marriage. Instead, through our friendship God gave me a safe environment to expose wounds and build my faith. I could lay my garbage out, sharing events which had filled me with shame for years. When I was finished, John would say, "That's nothing! Let me tell you about a day when I was twelve - I committed armed robbery an hour after my first sexual event."

It wasn't the easy fix I wanted, but God offered something simple: healing through a trusted friend. I have been able to be painfully honest with John, and together we have fallen on our knees in repentance. Again and again, John has pointed me to the cross. He has helped me believe the simple promise of God, "You are forgiven."

Part Five:

Brad

Boiled

The orthopedic surgeon pointed into the man's abdomen and said, "Hey, Tom, I can't make heads or tails out of it. What is that?"

I looked where he pointed and said, "That's poop."

"Why is there poop?"

Having just arrived in the operating room, I didn't know a thing, but I couldn't imagine it would matter much if I did. Half of the patient's body was missing from hip to ribs and he had feces throughout his pelvic region, I assumed he was septic and damn near dead. I asked the anesthesiologist, "How's he doing?"

"Stable," the anesthesiologist said. "He's doing fine."

He was stable, maybe, but fine was a stretch. The patient, I would later learn, was a thirty-nine year-old man named Brad who had spent most of his life in and out of California prisons. At the age of 36, he decided to start over in a new part of the country, away from familiar, destructive patterns. He moved out to the North Dakota plains where he met some good people and started a decent job.

Things were looking up until he shattered his leg in a four wheeler accident. He was an uninsured felon; he lost his job, and had nothing saved up, so he returned to what he knew: selling drugs. It was essentially the same business in North Dakota as it was in southern California, and it carried the same risks. It wasn't long before he was busted back to prison for three more years.

When he finished his time, he returned to North Dakota. His leg had healed up and his friends gave him a second chance at his old job. Again, things started looking up. He liked the work and met more good people. He moved into a nice house on a hill. He was on his way to a better life until one evening after dinner out with a friend he was walking with his dog towards home. As they crossed the railroad tracks, Brad noticed the slow moving train creeping toward them, but it was too far away to put them in any real danger. The movement of his dog, however, triggered an infrared safety mechanism, and its computer automatically switched the tracks in the exact spot Brad had just stepped. The rail pinched his left ankle, trapping his foot in place.

The train rolled towards him. Brad wrenched his body away, pulling back so hard he fractured his leg, but he couldn't free himself. He could only wait, bracing himself those last few seconds until steel frame of the train's engine sliced through him. In slow motion, it peeled the skin from his abdomen until his bowels were exposed. He had been eviscerated.

Many weeks later he described the next horrifying moments. "I was surprised to be alive at all," he said. "Then I was surprised to be standing. Then I saw my intestines hanging out… I don't remember anything after that."

They raced him to a hospital in North Dakota. There they found his pelvis had shattered, he had lost his abdominal wall and a large portion of his colon. It took several hours of surgery to wash him out. Then they closed him up and hoped for the best. Somehow, he survived the next few days, and even grew stable enough for the trip to my hospital in Saint Paul.

When he arrived his abdomen was a mess, filled with broken bones and organs - and there was the poop. It was because of this last that they paged me. When I joined them in the operating room, his abdomen was exposed so I could see parts of his bowel. I asked, "Where's your incision?"

"We don't have one," the orthopedic surgeon gestured to an area that stretched from hip to armpit, "That's all missing skin."

His body was twisted onto his side. The orthopedic team worked above on his pelvis so I had to move along the edge of the table - almost underneath him - in order to get to his abdomen. As I removed staples I realized his wound was just skin to skin. I slowly moved organs away to the point where my hand came out the very wound they were working on in the pelvis. I checked the colon reconstruction and found it had broken down - as a few percent do - and its contents were seeping into the belly. At this point I was able to form an idea of the injury. I understood the source of the contamination and I understood what I needed to do to stop it. But, given the way Brad was positioned, I would need to work upside down with my body twisted to get where I needed to be.

I was able to staple off each end of the colon which stopped the contamination. I brought the colon up through a separate wound in his upper quadrant and attached a colostomy bag. We dumped liters of saline into the wound then suctioned out the poop. We scrubbed the area until it was clean. We were successful in that his colon was no longer leaking and his abdomen was free of poop, but now we had to find a way to close the wounds if he were to have any chance of surviving.

Everyone has a big sheet of fat in their belly called the omentum. It is vascular and full of lymphatic tissue; we call it the watchdog of the abdomen. When a person gets an infection it moves and covers the problem area. If someone has appendicitis, for example, the omentum will shift towards that area. Or if someone had a perforated ulcer, the omentum will wiggle over and stick to it.

Brad was missing much of the inner structure of his abdominal wall, so we spread the omentum out as much as possible to cover his abdominal contents. We then used what skin we could find and tugged and stapled it together to make a temporary closure. Finally, when we had done all we could, we sent him to the ICU. He was in rough shape but alive.

Brad would go on to have fifty-five more operations. His pelvis and abdominal wall needed to be reconstructed. His belly and side were covered with skin grafts. He constantly battled infection.

In our trauma system, we bop around. Sometimes we will spend the week covering surgical ICU. Other times we will cover true trauma or emergency general surgery. Our connections with specific patients can be sporadic, so I only saw Brad a couple of times as he went through this process. After several months had passed, he had almost fallen off my radar when a nurse came flying into a workroom where John Turnipseed and I were having a conversation with a young man about LIFEteam. She yelled, "Oh my God! They're going to cut Brad's leg off!"

Brad's bones had shattered and most of the nerves to his left leg were ruined. He couldn't feel anything. He couldn't use the muscles. He was essentially dragging around a forty pound dead weight. Therefore the orthopedic surgeons had recommended amputation in order to prevent future wound issues like infections or ulcers.

John Turnipseed knew none of this, so he asked, "Who's Brad?"

I gave him the short version, "He's spent most of his life in prison for selling drugs. When he got out, he was hit by a train which shattered his pelvis. Now it looks like he might lose his leg."

"Hmm," John said. "My son lost his leg after being shot seventeen times. I have an idea of what Brad would be facing. Maybe I should talk to him."

The nurse said, "Well you better get in there now. It's so bad the orthopedic surgeon is praying for him."

We hurried to visit Brad but found the situation not quite as urgent as we were led to believe. Brad was a wreck, grieving over his leg, but the decision to remove it wasn't one he needed to act on immediately. He decided to wait, and, after some time passed and more healing, they ultimately made the decision not to amputate at all. But this episode led to John meeting Brad; and during that time I got to know him better as well.

I had been working with a different man from North Dakota at this same time who had been struggling with meth and crack cocaine. One afternoon I was reading and praying at home when my eye landed on the books sitting on our coffee table: a Bible I couldn't read because the print was too small, <u>Fight: Winning the Battles That Matter Most</u> by Craig Groeschel, and <u>Jesus>Religion</u> by Jefferson Bethke. I had been working on following prompts from the Holy Spirit so when something came to me that said, "Bring those books to the North Dakota guy," I listened.

Except the next morning I forgot and left the house without them. It wasn't until two days later when I was doing a 24 hour shift that I brought the three books with me. I went to the guy from North Dakota, the man addicted to meth, but he had been discharged. I had been sloppy the day before and now he was gone. Angry with myself, I cursed out loud to the empty room. Then, with those three books in my hand, I prayed, "Sorry God. I missed that one," and went on with my call shift.

Twenty hours later, after three o'clock the next morning, my resident called. "You need to come to the ER," he said. "This guy from North Dakota wants to talk to you."

I hurried downstairs to find 'the guy from North Dakota' was Brad - and he was in rough shape. He had a drug reaction called DRESS syndrome which shut down his bone morrow so he had no platelets in his blood. His kidneys were in failure. His heart rate was 140. His blood pressure was 80. The reaction had inflamed every inch of his skin. He was bright red, like he had been boiled in a microwave. His tattoos looked like they had been rubbed with sandpaper. He could tolerate contact with one square inch of skin on the palm of his hand, otherwise any touch caused him excruciating pain. He couldn't even bear bed sheets.

It was torture. In between sobs, he whimpered, "Tom."

I had to lean in to hear him. "Yeah, bud?"

"Kill me," he muttered. "I'm done."

"Brad, you know I can't do that."

"But you know me. Please. You can do it."

"Brad, we're at the point where there's only one thing I can offer."

Gently, I touched his palm. At this point I had never prayed out loud with another person, but I closed my eyes - I figured that was what you were supposed to do - and bumbled along using some of the words I had heard at church. I asked God to be there. I said something about Jesus. I mentioned healing several times. It was probably a 28 second prayer though it felt like a half hour.

When I looked up I saw Brad's face had relaxed. His eyes were shut. He was breathing softly. His pulse went down and his blood pressure went up so both were normal.

He had fallen asleep, and was - impossibly - at peace.

Nothing but Time

Later, Brad talked about this moment. "That was a point when nothing was working - not in my body, not in my life. It was all pain. When we prayed together, that was all I had. In that moment, I had to let go. In order to get through it, I knew I had to submit. I had to give up, and release everything to God."

Surrender. Brad had to do it, and so did I. This was the hardest lesson for me to learn, and the hardest for me to write about. As I enter into this story I know many who are reading will automatically be done, close the book, and give up on me - and I understand why. Two years ago I'm sure I would have done the same. Even though I denied the charges and they have all been dismissed, even though I was further examined by the medical board and cleared, still the stain will remain with me for a long time.

Out of respect for others involved, I will simply say that in early August of 2015, after an altercation with a family member, I found myself handcuffed in the backseat of a police car. They brought me to the station, gave me a shirt that didn't fit and sandals that rubbed at my feet like sand-paper. The pants were almost like scrubs except they were thick and itchy and smelled stale. So began the worst night of my life.

It was late, after midnight; the fluorescents in the book-ing room were buzzing and nothing felt real, as if I was living someone else's bad dream. I removed items from my pockets, my wrist watch, my car keys, but they seemed for-eign as if they belonged to a stranger - with one exception. As I pulled the cross from around my neck - the only time it had been off my body since I first received it - it had a shocking familiarity.

I laid the cross down and the booking officer spoke in a cold monotone, "Looks like you have a roommate."

In the middle of the buzzing nightmare, I heard a whis-per of God. I said, "I have the strangest feeling I'm sup-posed to talk to someone tonight."

I was thinking out loud more than anything else, but the booking officer asked, "What's that supposed to mean?"

He grabbed my cross from the desk and shoved it into a little envelope. I pointed, "It has something to do with that."

The man grunted, unimpressed. It was late, everything was locked down and quiet as I was led to my cell. It was little more than a concrete closet. There were two beds, a metal toilet and nothing else.

On the bottom bunk a kid who looked to be in his late-twenties was leaning up on his elbows watching me. His eyes looked hollow like they hadn't seen the sun for weeks.

"Sorry to wake you," I said.

"Don't worry. I can't sleep."

The door closed behind me. It wasn't particularly loud but I felt it in my chest when the lock engaged. In the dreadful silence, I quietly pleaded to God for peace. Then I introduced myself.

"You're not Tom Blee, the surgeon?"

I briefly considered hiding behind a lie, but shook it off and confessed. "Yes, I am."

"One of my best friends married your neighbor," he said. It is both a danger and blessing of living in a small town; the kid knew me. He told me his name was Andy and asked what I was doing there. I told the story as best I could.

He asked, "What are you going to do?"

"You know," I said, "there are times when all you can do is pray. All I've got right now is my faith. Everything else... I don't know."

He was friendly and he helped me set up my bed. The sheets came from the plastic bin I had been handed at the booking desk. It had basic toiletries and other necessities for jail life. I don't remember everything that was in it, but when I was released, prisoners kept asking me to look through it. They wanted the pencil or the comb or the toothpaste, whatever they could get.

After the bed had been made, there was nothing else to do, so I laid down and stared - eyes wide open - at the dark ceiling.

There was no way I was getting any sleep so it was a relief to hear Andy's voice. "Do you mind talking a bit?"

"I've got nothing but time."

"You mentioned faith before."

"It's all I've got."

He said, "I am lost." There was a quiet moment in which

I heard the thundering silence underneath the strange sounds of jail. "I am completely lost."

We talked for hours. He shared his story, his struggles, his pain, and I shared mine. He asked me about Jesus and I started on page one of the Bible: God created the universe. God created the earth. God created Adam and Eve. Then they screwed up and God worked to fix it. When the world grew to be a cess pool God sent Jesus - who loved us so much he died on a cross to save us.

It was hard to tell the time, but it was late, maybe four in the morning, when I finally said, "I've learned that when I don't know what to do, I should pray."

Andy said, "I don't know how."

"Why don't we pray together, then?"

And we did. I don't remember exactly what I said, but I prayed for Andy to get some rest; he hadn't slept in days. I prayed for protection. I prayed for comfort. I prayed for understanding. I went on until I heard a soft grumble from the lower bunk. Like Brad, Andy had fallen asleep in the middle of a prayer for peace - and he had begun to snore.

Buttons

Surrender. If you can do it before you lose everything, I'd recommend it. My night in jail marked the end of my marriage. I lost my place in the community and it threatened my livelihood. In that cell in the dark of night I felt like I had nothing left. Like Brad, I had no options except to give it all up to God.

In a strange way, surrendering is like learning to button a shirt. If you imagine the shirt represents your life then the top button needs to be God. He is your number one priority. The second button needs to be your spouse. The third is your kids. Down at the bottom, below all the others, is your career.

We get all screwed up when we mis-button our shirt. For me, throughout most of my adult life the top button had been my work as a surgeon. It gave me my identity. And sure, it messed up my shirt, but I liked it. I excelled at what I did so it made me comfortable. I was healing people which gave me respect from the community. Even after meeting Jesus in the white room, even after LIFEteam, even after learning from John Turnipseed, I still buttoned it all wrong. Honestly, it was all I knew. I wasn't even aware it needed to be changed.

But I was putting the bottom button on top. My sense of worth came from the operating room and not from God. And since I couldn't see it myself, there was only one fix: the shirt had to be ripped from my body. I needed to be stripped, torn down, destroyed. I needed to be brought to a place of total surrender. Only then could I be dressed in a completely new shirt. Only then would I be ready to receive my new identity, rooted not in myself but in Christ. It would be hard - I would have to relearn how to button it, and it wouldn't fit like the old one did. It would feel conspicuous at first - like a bad haircut. On my own I would never have done it, but in that jail I was given no other choice.

It was painful and humiliating, but once I let go and gave it all up to God, I experienced His grace in a way I could never have imagined.

In the Pit

At seven o'clock a guard woke us up for breakfast and I entered a whole new level of awful. When the doors opened I would no longer be able to hide in my cell. Dr. Tom Blee, Surgeon, had to come out of the darkness and face the flickering fluorescent lights of jail.

Andy rubbed sleep from his eyes. He looked better, more human. Before I said a word, he could tell I was afraid. "Don't worry, Tom," he said. "I've been here awhile. I'll show you what you need to do."

I have never felt so beaten down. I had no urge for anything. I didn't want to eat. I didn't want to drink. I didn't have an attorney or money to make the necessary phone calls. I had nothing but this scared kid who was willing to walk alongside me. I followed his lead with my head hanging so low my chin rested on my chest.

After picking at the mush which passed for breakfast we were given a few minutes to clean ourselves up. I was filthy but didn't have enough energy to shower. While Andy went off, I sat alone in the cell and stared at the floor.

I looked up only when he came back. His face was pale as he collapsed on the bunk next to me.

"I'm so nervous," he said, "I don't know what the hell is going to happen to me."

I felt like I was underwater. My brain barely worked but somehow I heard myself say, "Why don't we pray again?"

He nodded gratefully. "I was hoping you'd say that."

We prayed, but it wasn't me speaking; I had nothing left. I was empty. The words came from a deep place, and from somewhere - and Someone - outside of myself. As we asked for God's protection, a peace descended over our cell. Andy calmed and I felt a stirring of life grow in my belly. It wasn't much but it would give me strength enough to face the day.

They led me out for processing, which I quickly discovered was engineered for maximum frustration. Each moment grew more dehumanizing than the last. They sat me on a hard plastic bench in a windowless room, then handcuffed me to a rail next to a group of men. For a small town surgeon, it was bizarre. Some of the men had spent most of their adult lives incarcerated, others were experiencing it for the first time. One of them was a kid; he must have just turned eighteen. As the minutes dragged by, I listened to their banter.

"What are you in for?"

"Oh, plead this out. I've had that five times. That's nothing."

"Shit, I'm busted - I was out on parole. Now I'm gonna get stumped."

After an hour, they chucked me back into my cell. I had learned I would be standing before the court soon and regretted not showering. I had two days of stink on me and had spent the previous afternoon riding my mountain bike.

When they brought Andy back, he was so nervous his whole body shook. He had met with his attorney and his case did not look good. He paced for several minutes then stopped abruptly. "Tom," he sounded close to tears, "can we pray again?"

"Absolutely."

I started to pray but he interrupted me. "Hey Tom - all that stuff you talked about? Can we just get Jesus here for me? Can you invite that dude in?"

In jail I had been forced to surrender. The shirt I had buttoned so carefully my entire adult life had been ripped off and thrown away. I had one thing left - my faith in Jesus - and it was no coincidence it was the one thing Andy needed me to share. We sat next to each other on a dirty bunk in a closet of a cell and there I helped him invite Jesus into his life. I asked God to claim him, heal him, forgive him and make him new. I asked Jesus to bless him and protect him, and to walk with him through the difficult journey ahead.

When it was over, he smiled for the first time since I met him. He thanked me, thanked God, then soon was taken away for his court appearance. Later, he was released. In the year that has followed, we kept in touch. He's on a good path.

A few minutes later, it was my turn, and they sent me up to court in an elevator. My arms were in shackles. I didn't know where I was going or what would happen to me when I got there. I felt totally alone. As the elevator took me up, I was at the lowest I had ever been.

But when the guard brought me into the courtroom I

was greeted by familiar faces. There was John Turnipseed, his assistant Julie, and my sister Amy.

Amy is a woman of such strong faith and has an amazing Spirit-given gift of interpretation. Late the night before I had tried to call her from the jailhouse phone, but she was sleeping. When she woke she noticed the two strange phone numbers. She had a strange feeling that something was wrong with me and it prompted her to search for those numbers online. When she saw they originated from the Goodhue County Jail, she called John and cancelled her plans so I wouldn't have to face court alone.

I had thought I had no help. I had thought no one even knew I was there, but I was wrong. I was not alone in that courtroom, and looking back on the experience, I see I never was. In my lowest moment, at the edge of the valley of death, God was with me. He brought his angels to watch over me. Angels named Andy; angels named Amy; and angels named John and Julie[1]. It was God's way of saying again, "I've got you, Tom. Even here, even in the pit, even in the darkness, I've got you."

---

[1]   And angels named Paul and Adam. Even though we did not include the specifics of their story here, they showed up exactly when I needed them most.

The Glow

God makes 7000 promises in the Bible, and he doesn't break a single one. One of the biggest promises he has made to me is, "You do my work and I'll do yours. If you give me control of your life, I'm going to lead you through the darkness." I fought it every minute but finally in jail I was forced to surrender. The process was excruciating - it was the worst day of my life - but in return I experienced an intimacy with Jesus like I never had before. In that closeness was the true peace which passes understanding.

In his hospital room, every inch of his skin inflamed but one, Brad was also forced to surrender - and he also experienced a closeness with Jesus. Through a stumbling prayer, in the midst of tremendous pain, the peace of Christ enveloped him so fully he was able to sink into a blissful sleep.

I was away from the hospital for several days, but the day before I returned I heard a prompting from God: "Brad is your boy. He is the 'guy from North Dakota' who needs those books." It made sense so I grabbed them as I left the house. Later at the hospital I found Brad moving through dialysis and on a powerful antibiotic.

I asked, "How was the week?"

He had gone through hell, walking every day along the edge of the canyon of death. "It sucked," he said, but he was smiling. The inflammation had lessened and he wasn't in nearly as much pain. "But I'm doing okay."

Brad was with us for months, and as he slowly improved, I would visit him whenever I was on call. We discussed the books I had given him and had long talks about the Bible. I was no expert but shared what I knew. As with Andy in jail, I started on page one: God made the earth. God made Adam and Eve. They ate the fruit which screwed everything up, but God immediately started to fix it. He made the tree grow in the distance and then came down as Jesus.

Both of us looked forward to our talks. Brad soaked it up, hungry to learn all he could. It wasn't unusual for other patients or staff to listen in on our conversations and occasionally join in with a comment or question. It was a good time.

One afternoon, I was paged by the rehab unit. A nurse spoke in an urgent voice, "Doctor Blee, Brad needs you to come down here."

I was in the midst of a trauma resuscitation, but I ran down to him as soon as I was free. He wasn't in his room so I searched the hallways, but I couldn't find him there either. Finally, a nurse with a sly grin told me to check the stairwell.

I opened the door she had indicated and there was Brad. He wore a brace and needed help from a physical therapist but he was climbing a flight of stairs on the same leg that at one point was scheduled to be cut off. He beamed up at me, "Look doc!" he shouted. "Isn't this amazing?"

It was more than amazing. I said, "That's unbelievable."

He laughed, "It's a God-thing, isn't it?"

It absolutely was.

Later, back in his room, he told me he was finally going home - which wasn't necessarily good news. His personal life was still a mess. He was divorced. His son didn't like him. His step-daughter wanted little to do with him. It was going to be a rough road, but in that moment he was at peace. He had an inner light which brightened the room. "Tom," he said, "I've got that same glow that you and John have - I can feel it."

Brad had to lose everything: his family, his livelihood, and his health; he had to be stripped down to nothing before he finally surrendered. "In order to get through it," he reflected later, "I knew I had to let go. I had to give it all up to God."

When he did, he found Jesus waiting there for him. "I was such a piece of shit my whole life but you and John just kept coming back. You just kept showing up and telling me about Jesus. And because of that, I knew Jesus cared. I knew he loved me and I wasn't going to let him down."

Surrender. Letting go of yourself and trusting fully in Jesus. It may be the most difficult part of following him, but - when you finally lose yourself and feel him catch you, hold you, lift you up - there is nothing more glorious.

Part Six:

Kiowa

Chiseled

Kiowa came in at two in the morning with a stab wound to his chest. He was angry, filling the room with furious noise. A big guy, well over six feet and chiseled out of steel, he could be an imposing character, especially sputtering with rage - but something was different about him. He didn't frighten us.

Something was different about me as well. It had been less than a week since I had been out of jail, and my thinking had changed. Kiowa kept shouting, "I didn't do it!" and I believed him.

I see injuries like his every day and can distinguish the differences between them. His wound appeared to have happened while he was defending himself. On top of this, the other party involved was sitting in the ER with a set of wounds which confirmed Kiowa's innocence.

Typically when the evaluation is done I would move from the trauma bay and onto the next patient, but I didn't want to leave Kiowa alone. A police officer was there, asking for the standard information and giving Kiowa forms to sign. I started to coach him. I told him which form he needed to sign and which he didn't. I asked, "Do you have to take his cell phone?"

The police officer shook his head no. This was good for Kiowa but it also gave me an opportunity. With a cell phone, I could connect with him right away through texting.

Kiowa appreciated my help but he was worked up. I tried to connect him to LIFEteam, but he wasn't able to hear me in the moment. He was distracted by the chaos, and wasn't ready to trust some strange doctor. This was a problem as we didn't have much time. His injury wasn't bad - he had a small hole in his lung but was expected to recover without any trouble - and he would be discharged the next morning. Throughout the night I stopped in to check on him, and bit by bit he calmed down. But he remained too guarded for me to reach.

The night passed and morning came but I still hadn't made a connection with Kiowa. Everything was looking good medically, he was able to go home, so I figured I had one last chance. I sat down near his bed. "Listen, Kiowa," I said. "Here is where you stand." I told him frankly what I saw in his situation, both medically and legally. Then I told him about my own recent experience spending a night in jail.

It was the first time I had spoken about it to anyone besides my sister and John. To be honest, it hurt. I felt exposed, afraid someone might overhear, wondering what this guy was thinking of me.

Throwing Garbage

Surgeons fix things, and because of that there are some who assume we must not have problems of our own. For much of my life I worked hard to preserve this illusion. But then I went to jail, then my marriage fell apart, then I was forced to surrender everything to God. It hurt to get here, but I've finally learned to be honest about my struggles: I am dented, I am dinged, and my path is filled with chaos. It is never easy, but speaking this truth has brought me closer to Christ.

John Turnipseed taught me that it can also be a powerful tool in my toolbox. My brokenness is a connection point with some of these young men who come through our trauma system. Growing up in the chaos of alcoholism was a nightmare, spending a day in jail was awful, but God has worked through these experiences to open doors. Injured men allow me in the room because I'm a surgeon, but after I fix them I can talk simply as a guy who went through some of the same kinds of trouble.

Recently, leaders from another hospital asked John

and me about what makes our program work. We said, "It works because we tell the truth. We throw our garbage out there."

An intervention specialist with excellent training will have some success, but if we're not in the dirt with those we are trying to help, they won't see anything real. If we are not in the grind with them, they will listen to our Ten Ways to Healthy Living with a shrug. But if we can be honest with them about the world of crap we have slogged through ourselves, then they will see we have something more than words to offer. We can give them hope.

Wake-up Call

Kiowa's eyes grew big as I shared my story. Finally he began to drop his guard. Speaking honestly about my own dirt got through to him and from that moment, we became friends.

At first, I looked at our connection in the wrong way. I would soon learn his nickname was JobCore because he tends to his neighborhood by doing odd jobs, fixing cars, mowing lawns, and helping people wherever he can. He earns money through a complicated barter system. He is a doer and a fixer, but as we had our first real conversation, my only thought was, "What do I need to do to help this guy?" This was the wrong question. God brought Kiowa into my life to help me.

Kiowa had been to hell and back, but from the beginning he kept pushing the conversation onto me. As the weeks went by, he'd ask about my sons and coach me as one dad to another. He'd say, "What do you need? How can I help?" He quickly became a trusted friend and confidant. He joined my family for Easter. It became a relationship that was bigger than me, bigger than us: he became a strange and remarkable part of the symphony which could have only been orchestrated by God.

Sometimes things grow so dark, we can't see a way out. Three months after we met, I called him the night before I was facing a morning in court. I was reeling, in disbelief that any of it had happened at all. All the charges were going to be dismissed, but I still felt nervous. My anxiety clouded my vision so in the moment I couldn't see Jesus. I couldn't see God at work. I couldn't see that tree growing in the garden: the cross of Christ.

Kiowa could read me easily and before we had said much of anything he asked, "What's the matter?"

"It's… this thing tomorrow. I don't know what's going to happen."

"What time is court?"

"Supposed to be at 9:30."

"Listen," he said. "This is barely a court case. All it is - it's an early morning wake-up call. You get there and you're going to be fine." He said it again, "Tom, this is nothing but an early morning wake-up call."

He spoke with an authority that cleared away the anxiety. It was just a few words but it gave me the encouragement I needed. I could again see clearly that Jesus was at work in the situation. I was at peace.

After our conversation, I sat for awhile and talked to God. I gave him thanks for surrounding with me good people - men and women who walk with me every step of the way. As I prayed, I had a startling realization: LIFE-team had been ministering faithfully to me for the past two years. I was the first client.

First Client

The idea of LIFEteam is to engage with people at their most vulnerable and offer them the help and care they need to get on the path to true healing. With Tay and Brad and many others we found the program could be successful in changing lives. However, for everyone trying to start a new life - particularly when they are caught up in gangs - the first two years can be deadly. Gangs are toxic but they offer these men community, identity and protection - and apart from them, our LIFEteam clients feel lost and vulnerable. It is critical that they have someone to walk with them through those first years. We need to surround them with a new community, and point them towards a new identity. This protects them because it communicates to the gangs: "He's not one of yours anymore - don't touch him." If our clients don't have these things - community, identity and protection - they will often slip back into that comfortable noise, no matter how deadly. They go back to what they know, even if it's chaos.

The physical details of my situation and a typical LIFEteam client could not be more different - I know that. I didn't have to get off drugs or escape gang life. Still, in a similar way, I too needed to move from the darkness to the light. I needed to escape toxic patterns. I needed to shed an old identity and embrace a new one. And, like it has been for the rest of our clients, the first two years for me were absolute hell.

Some Christian teachers make it sound like you start following Jesus and everything gets better. Life gets easy. Everything just starts to work out. And maybe this is how it works for some, but it was not my experience. God gave me a few months after the white room to walk with Jesus and learn about him, but it wasn't long before He said, "It's time to be tested and tempered. I'm bringing you down into that valley. Things are about to get rough."

It has been the most difficult time of my life, but as we did for each of our clients, so LIFEteam did for me. They surrounded me each step of the way with love. They mentored me through difficult decisions. They reminded me when needed of my identity in Christ.

My sister Amy walked me through that first night in the white room. John Turnipseed showed up two months later. A group of men at church became the Beer and Banter boys and we met weekly to talk about Jesus and scripture. Brad, Tay, Andy and finally Kiowa - men with completely different backgrounds and toolboxes - showed up exactly when and where I needed them. Through my worst moments, my darkest and most difficult times, God never left me alone. He used LIFEteam to walk with me into impossible healing.

Who's Joe?

Impossible healing, through a free gift of God's grace, is not a passive process. We are not called to lounge back and receive God's blessings like we are luxuriating at a spa. No, as we are being healed, Jesus calls us out to be his angels and heal others. God sent Kiowa to care for me in my time of need, but the relationship went both ways. I was pushed out of my safe zone and into Kiowa's world as well.

A few months after we met, Kiowa had a job interview lined up when someone had been murdered in the alley behind his building. The area became a crime zone and police and press crowded the streets. He had no way of getting to his truck.

He explained his dilemma to me on the phone as I drove towards home. My initial thought was he should simply reschedule the job interview. I started to say as much when I had this piercing sense that God expected more. I drove quietly for a few moments in prayer. I felt God wanted me to step up - like He was saying, "Tom, it's time to push it."

"Kiowa, I'll be there as soon as I can," I said as I navigated a complicated U-turn on a four lane road. I hung up, and then, as I drove towards a murder scene in the inner city after dark, I made a quick call to my sister.

"You can't go," she said.

I shared her concern. We grew up in a modest Minnesota town and to this day I still think of myself as more farmer than surgeon - but none of that mattered. God wasn't giving me a choice. "I have to," I said. "So start praying."

I pulled up to Kiowa's street and found the area completely pinned down. Crime tape draped the sidewalk and there were more cop cars than I'd ever seen in one place. News vans were lined up back to back. I parked as close as I could - which was several blocks away - and hurried to the scene. I had built many connections with the gang unit so I started making phone calls but no one answered. I knew some reporters, but I didn't recognize any of the ones nearby.

There was nothing else to be done, so I skirted around the crime scene, followed a dark street for a half-block, and found Kiowa's address. It was a dreary night in early November; dismal and misting without quite raining. The building was dark: every light on his front porch was busted. I felt strangely small and vulnerable, like I was intruding where I was not wanted. Twelve feet from the back door of this apartment was a dead body. The neon lights of the cop cars shined from around the corner. I couldn't help but think, "What am I doing here?"

I dialed Kiowa's number but he didn't answer so I pounded on the door, not sure if anyone was there to hear it. For several long minutes I could do nothing but shiver in the darkness. Eventually an old Cadillac inched up behind me. The headlights went out and I could only see shadows move behind the tinted glass. Then the glow of a cigarette. Finally, a strange man climbed out, then after a moment a woman followed. I nodded at them, said, "Good evening," but they didn't say anything as they stepped onto the porch. They stood near, silent, waiting for something. I felt like a trespasser in a world with rules and rituals I couldn't understand.

Another minute went by in silence before Kiowa finally burst out in a rush. He nodded friendly to my porch-mates then said, "We gotta get going."

We hurried to my car. I asked him, "You all right?"

"I'm fine, let's move."

"There's a body in your back yard."

He shrugged, unfazed. "Yeah, they blocked me in." It was clear that things like this had happened enough that they had become more an inconvenience than a tragedy.

Here's the thing about impossible healing: God orchestrates it in ways that will often blow your mind. And so it was that Kiowa and I - about as unlikely a duo as one could imagine - drove across the city together on a rainy November evening. We pulled up to a shipping business in an industrial park. To add to the strangeness of the evening, we found all the employees sitting in a back parking lot. They were having a fire drill.

I asked Kiowa, "Who are you supposed to talk to?"

"Some dude named Joe."

I called to the crowd, "Who's Joe?"

Every head went straight down. Remember, Kiowa is a huge man, well over six feet tall and all muscle - no one wanted to get entangled with him. Trying a different approach, I said, "We're here for a job interview. Can someone tell me where we can find Joe?"

From the middle of the crowd, a man stood up. "I'm Joe."

Kiowa said, "I'm here for a job interview."

Joe looked at me. "Who are you?"

"I'm Kiowa's friend."

He eyed Kiowa, "And who are you?"

Kiowa smiled. "I'm Dr. Tom's friend."

Joe took us back and had Kiowa fill out various forms. As he did that, I peppered one of their guys from HR with questions. When the guy left, I was able to tell Kiowa about the company, the basics about the job opening, and give him some questions to ask.

He was called back and I sat in this locked lobby which reminded me painfully of a jail cell. It was about the same size with concrete walls and one little bathroom. I took a quiet moment and offered a prayer of thanks to God. Nothing about following Jesus had been easy. Still, it was amazing to sit there in that dark and quiet room, knowing that God had led me into Kiowa's world as Kiowa had been led into mine. It was an impossible friendship which led to impossible healing for both of us. I gave thanks for how simple it was - follow Jesus and he will make things glorious. Sure, it can be strange. He may surround you with the most ragtag group of nut-balls you can imagine. He may demand you do things you never thought you would be equipped to do - but in the end it will be absolutely amazing.

Twenty minutes later Kiowa came out smiling ear to ear. The next day they offered him the job.

Part Seven:

Nada

That Boy's Okay

Nada was a whole four foot nine and 86 years old when she walked into my office. Considering her age, I looked at one thing on her chart - anemia - and thought, "She has cancer."

It appeared to be a clear cut case, except when I told her my suspicions and that we needed to test for cancer of the colon, she shook her head. "I'm not doing anything," she said. "I'm not drinking that nasty stuff. No way."

Nada, I would learn, was a formidable woman. Born in Yugoslavia, she made the firm decision in her twenties to leave everything she knew and immigrate to Red Wing where she married the owner of a local candy store. A woman of courage her whole life, she was never one to back down.

I listened seriously to her concerns. When she was done, I knew I needed to be blunt. "Nada," I said, "with your age and symptoms, this is cancer unless proven otherwise." I spoke clearly of the suffering she could expect to experience if she didn't seek treatment.

She thought about it for a day or two then agreed to get tested. It came back positive. She needed surgery.

We are always concerned with women of her age with what we were going to find when we get her to the operating room, and for Nada, it turned out to be the worst case scenario: Fungating cancer nearly blocking her colon. It had spread to her stomach and part of her small intestine. Seeing it, I scrubbed out quickly to talk to her daughter and son. "This thing is big," I told them. "It has to come out in a block, along with anything it touches."

It ended up being a six and a half hour operation. We did a colon resection, a partial stomach resection, then a small intestine resection. In the best case scenario she would have one hookup inside and there would be a 2-5% chance that it would leak. Nada had three different hookups: on her stomach, small intestine and colon. For Nada, at 86 years old, it was especially dangerous.

She was moved to the intensive care unit. The first day she struggled in the typical way. Two days later, however, I found her walking around the halls. Nada had a magic - a presence - and by this point the whole staff was letting her do whatever she wanted. When I tried to intercept her she batted me away. "This is fine," she said. "It's not a problem."

She needed to be discharged to a transitional care unit to finish her recovery. She was reluctant, but since she lived on her own we were insistent. After a long discussion with her family, she finally consented.

First thing the next morning, she left the hospital for an indefinite stay in a local nursing home. We said our good-byes and I went to tend another patient. I assumed, of course, I wouldn't see her for some time unless there was an emergency, but an hour later a nurse stopped in my office. She told me, "Nada is here."

Confused, I said, "No, she just left."

The nurse shrugged. "See for yourself." She gestured, and yes, there was Nada sitting outside my office gripping a stack of papers. She swung them under my chin.

"You're going to sign these right now."

"What are they?"

"These are my discharge papers. I'm going home."

"But Nada," I said. "You can't! You just had major surgery."

"I'm fine. I can do everything I have to do at home." I was almost a foot taller than she was, but she stared me down. "Sign the papers." She handed me a pen and pointed to the line.

For a brief moment I considered putting up a fight. I thought of how I might insist she return immediately to the care facility. But then I saw the look in her eyes and I knew I had already lost.

"Thank you," she said as I signed the papers. Her stern demeanor softened into a grin. "Now give me a picture."

"Of what?"

She glared at me like I hadn't been paying attention. "Of your family."

"For what?"

"For a cross-stitch."

I had no idea what she was talking about, but I knew she wouldn't quit bothering me until she got what she wanted, so I raised my hands in surrender. "Okay, okay. I'll get you a picture."

Two weeks later she came in for a check up. According to her pathology report, she probably needed chemotherapy.

"I'm not doing chemotherapy," she said. "Now where is that picture?"

I didn't have one, but when I saw her on my calendar for her six week follow up, I ran home for a wallet-sized photo of my two sons. She giggled in her chair when she saw it. She had no interest in talking about the cancer, but then discussions with Nada were never about Nada. She was a person who wasn't focused on herself. Even in the examination room, she would interrupt with, "What is going on with you?"

I gave her the picture and I forgot about it until - five months later - there was a knock on my front door. Through the window I could see an adult and a child. I expected Girl Scouts or Mormons, but the child of course was no child; it was Nada, and the 'adult' was her daughter.

She didn't wait for an invitation. "Your picture's done," she said as she walked into my house. She made herself comfortable on my living room couch then futzed with a tube. After a little tugging, she unraveled a cross-stitched portrait of my boys.

It was beautiful and intricately detailed. Before I could express anything but astonishment, she started explaining my two sons to me. The boys are very different from each other. One is more boisterous, the other more gentle. After spending months on this project, studying that photograph, Nada had nailed it. She spoke of them as if she had known them her whole life.

With that, she gave me the cross-stitch, said thank you for doing the surgery, and left.

My family and I treasured the portrait, but Nada's path and mine didn't cross again until the winter of that year. In December we received the news that Harry Exner, a family friend, had been struck and killed by a light rail train in Denver, Colorado. He was nineteen years old, and had been on a great path, a remarkable person. It was an unGodly, unexplainable, unimaginably tragic event. It was a nightmare for the family and a time of grief for the whole community.

In the days that followed, it felt impossible to take the next breath. I didn't know what to say to his family; it all seemed too big, but when I went to his funeral Nada and her cross-stitches kept coming into my head.

I explained the situation to Nada and she thought for a long moment. The moment contained something I would recognize later in that white room on my knees: a thundering silence. Finally, she said, "I feel their pain," then continued almost in a whisper, "I'll do it."

I gave her Harry's photo and went back to my life. I went to work, came home, returned to the daily routine. The world continued to turn, but in her little room at the Jordan Towers late at night, often until two or three in the morning, Nada was working. It was, in a way, quite simple. It didn't take years of study or any highly-specialized skills. When God heals, he doesn't need any of that stuff. No, the greatest healer I ever knew worked prayerfully in her chair, quietly cross-stitching in the long hours after The Tonight Show was over.

It took several months but she called me as soon as she finished. It had been a little photograph, two inches square, but she had made it into a grand portrait. The whole thing was beautiful, but, most strikingly, Nada gave a gentle expression to the young man's eyes which said, "I'm still with you."

"Nada," I told her, "this is amazing."

She didn't seem to hear me, but said, "That boy's okay."
"What do you mean?"

She gazed at me, speaking with her peculiar authority, "That boy's okay." Then, as she did with my sons, Nada explained Harry's heart. She shared her own grief and affection she had felt as she worked on the portrait.

The family was in tears when they received it; it was a beautiful moment. In God's surprising way, He orchestrated the connection of a ninety year-old immigrant - with all the miles that she had walked - to a grieving family. He put everyone together in a single moment overflowing with impossible healing.

Midnight Cross-stitch

My encounter with Nada happened years before my encounter with Jesus in the white room. I wasn't ready to see it at the time, but God put her in my life to help open my eyes. God was showing me what it looks like to be a true healer - someone who doesn't point to herself but uses her toolbox to help everyone around her.

It was a lesson I needed to learn. My professional life is centered around being in careful control of situations filled with chaos. Because of its very nature, I would take all of the responsibility onto myself. Frankly, there's a certain pleasure in this. It feels good to put ourselves at the center of healing. It is comforting, like the shirt we have buttoned the wrong way. But it is terribly heavy as well.

It hurts to think, "I did everything right so what went wrong?" Why did the young woman live who had been crushed by a dump truck? Why did the other woman die after falling from a slow moving car? The honest answer is 'I don't know,' but the burden of that mystery can be over-whelming when you think you are the one in control.

Of course this sense of control is all a delusion. In reality, the ultimate controller of life, death and healing is bigger than me. It is bigger than all the teams and systems that surround me.

In truth, no matter our perceptions in the moment, God is calling all the shots and healing is happening. In our limited way, we may not see it in the moment, but his healing is bigger and beyond what any of us could dream up.

Ultimately, it is not about the surgeon. This is what Nada taught me. In Christ, healing, true healing - impossible healing - happens beyond the operating room. It happens in surprising ways and places - including the living room of a tiny woman cross-stitching at midnight. When our eyes are open to this truth, we can be free. We don't have to lug that burden around anymore. God is in control and we can relax and trust him. This freedom makes us better parents, better spouses, better friends. In the end, since we are engaging the true source of healing, it frees us to become better healers ourselves.

Nada helped show me the way. She pointed to the Impossible Healer before I was ready to see him.

The Emmy

Nada had offered her gifts to a family in need and I wanted to offer her something in return. This proved to be a challenge because Nada would likely refuse any physical gift. It was a puzzle I wrestled with for weeks until, strangely, Boyd Huppert came to mind. He was a reporter who wrote features for the local NBC affiliate, KARE 11. I thought he could do a story on her, but I had no connection with him. Finally, after I had no other ideas, I sent an email to his address on their website. In it, I told him about Nada and the healing she offers through her art.

I braced myself for a wait, figuring there would be some torturous process through various interns and assistants. It was a surprise, then, when only a couple days later I received an email from Boyd himself. It read, "Absolutely! I would love to do it."

He did a story on Nada, calling her "Red Wing's Angel." As part of it, we gathered her cross-stitches and brought them back to her. The people she has impacted met with her in a community room at her apartment complex. It was a joyful afternoon filled with thanksgiving.

I arrived after it had already begun and found Nada holding court with her admirers. She called my name when she saw me and we goofed with each other for a few moments - if anyone said anything mildly funny she always busted out with an infectious laugh. Then I looked around at the people who had been touched by her gift, and I said, "You know Nada, I fix people but you heal them."

The story came out beautifully[1] and Boyd Huppert won an Emmy for it. In an act of tremendous generosity, he gave the statue to Nada.

Some time later, before I left my surgical practice in Red Wing, the second to last person I operated on was Nada. Her gall bladder needed to come out and she called me to do it. I said, "Nada I'm not operating any more. I can't. It's the way you wind down a practice."

"Well," she answered. "You can end with me."

"But Nada…"

"You can end with me."

We scheduled her surgery.

First thing in the morning I went to Nada's room to do the prep work, but she wasn't there. I asked the nurses in the pre-op area where she had gone and they laughed. One finally told me, "She's walking around the building. She brought her Emmy and she's showing it off."

Typically, because they are so expensive to run, any delay in the operating room regardless of the reason is not tolerated. But for Nada, what can you do? She would take as much time as she needed. She could walk around that hospital fourteen times, and it wouldn't be a problem.

---

1   You can find her story by going to www.kare11.com and searching for 'Nada.'

I finally found her upstairs in the ICU. She was explaining her Emmy to the nurses, who were all delighted to see her. Her daughter was walking behind her holding the gown together. After telling her story three more times, she finally acknowledged me. With a wink, she said, "I'm ready for surgery now."

A part of me wanted to say, "My operating room's been wide open for an hour," but I just laughed and led her back to the pre-op area.

This time the risk was in many ways greater than the first surgery. She was older and had undergone a six hour operation to remove the cancer. I expected the inside of her abdomen to be covered in scar tissue, like a bomb had gone off. Instead, I made the incision, turned on the camera and it looked pristine - like it had never been touched.

We finished the operation in forty-five minutes. Nada woke up, took her Emmy, and went home.

Moving Day

It happens throughout the scriptures: God takes some-thing nasty and turns it into something amazing. For Nada, God took her cancer and turned it into an Emmy.

It happens all around us every day; we just have to open our eyes to see it. I was blessed by one of these miracles in my own life when God took one of my worst days and turned into a time of healing.

It was the first weekend of July, 2016, and I was pulling up to my old house for the last time. It was the place my sons grew up. It was a place of happier memories from my marriage. It was the place I fell to my knees and prayed to God. It had been a good home - but it was also a place full of pain. It was a place where a marriage broke down into bitter regrets and tense silences. It was a place filled with soured memories.

It was time to move.

Still, after all that happened over the past year, this was one of the most traumatic: walking back into that mostly empty house, gathering the last bits of my stuff and piling them into the truck. After all the life I had invested into that home, the process of leaving felt a lot like death.

Thank God I wasn't alone. For the past two years I had been gathering with a group from church every Tuesday night. Called Beer and Banter, it was founded by a man named John and currently led by a retired truck driver named George. Their mantra was: If you're going to be a fisher of men, better use the right bait. For that group the right bait was beer. They were a bunch of small town men gathering every week to talk about Jesus. Peter, John, John, Terry, Orv, Larry, Bruce, Brad, Mike, Russ and Russ, many of them arrived at my old house to help. My sister, Amy, was there and our friend, Lisa. It was a ragtag bunch only God could put together. They were a gift, a reminder, a way for Jesus to say, "I'm here. That's just a house, and I'll send some of my people to help you get out of it. Just do my work, Tom, and I'll do yours."

In the house was a mixture of memories and garbage, sometimes in the same drawer. In one cabinet I found a framed picture of our family sitting next to a broken pump from a forgotten fountain. I stared at it for a long moment. It seemed somehow a perfect metaphor for the last two years of my life.

I considered the journey which had brought me to that moment. I remembered the night I fell on my knees in prayer. I remembered my first meeting with John Turnipseed, the beginning of LIFEteam, the excitement of following Jesus. I remembered seeing how huge He was - His love was so much bigger than anything I ever dreamed. I remembered the amazing healing; God orchestrating these impossible moments of grace. And in the midst of it all, here was this brokenness, this hurting, this crumbling marriage, this house filled with heartache.

It was amazing to have the guys there to help me move. We had fun as we worked. One of the guys - his name happened to be Peter - would disappear every hour or so and come back with a twelve pack of beer. But when I went out with the picture in one hand and the broken pump in the other, no one made any jokes. They knew I was hurting. My boys surrounded me, my sister placed her hand on my shoulder, and we prayed.

It was a powerful moment. Again, I was reminded that God kept sending his angels. John Turnipseed, Brad, Andy, Kiowa, Nada, these Beer and Banter boys. Every time I would hit my lowest point, Jesus would surround me with people to lift me up.

And once again, as he did for Caitlyn and Brad and Tay - as he turned Nada's cancer into an Emmy - God took the broken remnants of my marriage and built a glorious moment of impossible healing.

I held that photograph and that piece of garbage and I prayed. I owned up to my own faults, my own culpability, my own sin. In the midst of the hurt and anger of divorce, it was an act of surrender just as difficult as anything I experienced in jail. But surrounded by my friends I experienced the peace of knowing that Christ took all my failures to the cross. In his death I was forgiven.

Without forgiveness, we're done. We would have been done from the start. Adam and Eve would have had no chance of turning around and seeing the cross. They would have been stuck looking the wrong way. Without forgiveness we would have nothing but the easy answers of empty apologies. Without forgiveness I could never turn away from my wounds - both those that I have caused and those that have been done to me.

Forgiveness is the ultimate impossible healing. In Christ we can turn away from that wound, give it to God, and watch as he covers it with his blood to make us whole.

Praying with my friends, I knew - I experienced it - that in Christ, I was forgiven. And there, held in God's hands, I could safely look back on my life, my childhood, my rivalries, and my marriage. I could reflect back on a life filled with the same dings and hurts as any other, and see it filled with God's grace. I could forgive those who hurt me, knowing we are all broken. We are all petty. We are all scratching to get through another day. With few exceptions like Nada we all spend too much time looking at ourselves instead of God. We are each sinners, but the Impossible Healer is bigger than all of it. He can turn cancer into an Emmy. He can turn a day of sorrow into a day of grace. He can turn this poor sinner into one of his saints.

It wasn't easy, but it was beyond anything we could orchestrate. It was the power of the blood of Christ healing me again, making me and all things new. Ultimately, standing in the driveway in front of a house that was no longer my home, the blood of Jesus turned that anguished prayer of lament into a joyful prayer of thanks.

Jesus is doing the same thing in your life right now. He is sending your own angels, your own Nada, your own John Turnipseed. He is loving you, waiting for you to engage, wanting nothing more than to pour impossible healing into your life as well. You don't need any fancy skills, you don't need to be perfect. In fact, sometimes those things will often only get in your way. No - the only thing you need is Jesus.

Next Steps

Day of Prayer

I am a healer by trade and temperament, so as I have gone through this journey I kept thinking: How can others experience this? It's so good, how do I share it with the world?

I am at a teaching hospital and I always tell my residents the same thing. When you leave here, you will have learned about 80% of what you will need to know. The other 20% will only come from experience and judgement.

For example, recently we had a patient in our ICU. She was very sick and we needed to make a hard decision. Do we bring her into the operating room and remove all of her colon and half of her small intestines? She would survive the immediate crisis but then not have enough gut to eat. Or do we wait? Waiting could lead to dead bowel which would be catastrophic. It is a difficult situation and one the surgeon faces almost every day. Still, we have to make the call. As hard as it might be, that is our job.

In this particular patient's situation, it was my judgement to wait. Every hour I checked, looking for more data - and every hour I prayed. Finally, after sixteen hours the patient improved to a point where surgery was unnecessary. In the end, I had made the right decision, but it was a fearsome place to be.

It would have been worse if I didn't have God there, which is why recently I have been wondering: What if you brought God in? So we have 80% training and 20% experience and judgment. Now imagine we had 1% of God. For

Moses, 1% of the presence of God made him glow. What would it do in a hospital? Imagine you have a ten person team in the trauma bay and one person is praying. What would happen? Imagine the whole ICU team was praying. Imagine if we have an internal website firing prayers to groups throughout the community - or the city - or around the world. It could change the hospital. It could change the definition of true healing.

But let's think even bigger. Imagine if we joined together - you take whatever ragtag group of nut-balls God has placed in your path - and I take mine and we gather with them to pray - for the hurting and the sick and the vulnerable. Imagine a day of prayer for health care workers. Imagine how powerful that would be: people meeting, talking and praying together. Imagine if you let God lead you and your own LIFEteam into the dark corners of the world to bring true healing to those who need it. Imagine teams of people around the world engaging with God. They could do the impossible. They could change the world.

To sign up for our mailing list and receive more information on the Day of Prayer for Health Care Workers, connect with us at www.howtosaveasurgeon.com.

Again and Again

The first thing we teach in advanced trauma life support is the ABCs: Airway - Breathing - Circulation. And no matter how many years you have been a doctor, you can never forget it. It always comes back. When you don't know what to do in the midst of a medical catastrophe you focus on the ABCs.

This person is missing half their body. That one is screaming and vomiting. Family members are crying for help. Here is a veterinarian offering to assist. There's noise and fear and chaos. You can get distracted by a dozen things.

But it all comes down to this: Do you have an airway? Are you breathing? How do I get circulation? A-B-C.

If my story moved you, if it stirred something either dormant or forgotten in your soul, then you may find yourself in a similar position I was when I stood up from my knees in the white room.

You have had an experience with Jesus, but it has left you confused. You haven't any training for this. You have no idea what to do next. The world offers a thousand options. It is filled with noise and chaos. You could follow a hundred ministers, read a thousand books. It can be overwhelming.

But it all comes down to this: The ABCs.

Admit you need help. Admit you're wounded and a band-aid is not going to help - you need a blood transfusion.

Believe that God is there to help us and love us. Believe that Jesus has his arms wide open for you.
And

Commit yourself to Christ. Commit to getting to know him. Commit to keeping it simple and following Jesus on whatever crazy journey he has planned for you.

And that's it. A-B-C. It will not be easy. At times it will be darker and more difficult than any other time in your life. But Jesus will walk every step of the journey with you. And if you lose your way, if you get lost in the dark and the noise of the world threatens to overwhelm you again? Keep it simple. Go back to the ABCs:

Admit.

Believe.

Commit.

Over the past two years I have had to do it again and again. And it has been far from easy, but through the simple grace of God I can now say to the gang-banger with a bullet through his belly to the trauma surgeon working to fix him, and to absolutely everyone who is reading this book: Turn to him. Admit you need help. Believe in his promises. Follow where he leads. No matter how damaged, Jesus can heal you. I know this because he is healing me.

Get Involved

If anything in this book has moved you to action then check out any of these excellent organizations. They are each deserving your support:

Neighborhood House of St Paul

Website: www.neighb.org

About: "When families and individuals in St. Paul want to make a change in their lives, Neighborhood House is there to help. We are a multi-service agency, providing wrap-around services for people when they need it most. Neighborhood House helps people with basic needs, education, multiple youth programs, and health and well-being. All of our programs are offered for free to participants."

GRIP: Gang reduction Intervention Program

Website: www.neighb.org/programs/grip/

About: "We help youth define their identity, make positive contributions to the community, build upon personal strengths/interests, and increase community support systems in their lives. We serve youth ages 11-24. These youth are either currently involved in the juvenile justice system or at risk of becoming involved."

Urban Ventures of Minneapolis

Website: www.urbanventures.org

About: Urban poverty is complex. And it's close to home. Generations of families living in the urban core lack access to economic, educational, spiritual, and social capital. Systemic cycles of generational poverty breed hopelessness.Urban Ventures exists to close the gaps that perpetuate urban poverty.

Center for Fathering

Website: www.urbanventures.org/program-directory

About: The Center for Fathering works to empower men and women to be effective and loving parents through engaging large and small group classes. Each session is taught by urban parenting experts and focuses on teaching practical skills, helping participants be the parent their children need.

Ujaama Place of St Paul

Website: www.ujamaaplace.org

About: Ujamaa Place is an African American culturally specific organization focused on young men who may suffer multiple barriers to becoming stable. Ujamaa Place engages these young men to foster their development within the Ujamaa Place community and assist them in becoming stronger, more responsible, employed, prosperous men and fathers who provide and contribute positively to their families and community.

The Second Prison Project

Website: www.prisonfellowship.org

About: Jesse Wiese and the Second Prison Project work to eliminate the "second prison" of social and legal barriers that prevent millions of Americans with a criminal record from reaching their highest potential.

St Paul YWCA (programs of Joe Lash)

Website: www.ywcaofstpaul.org

About: YWCA St. Paul is dedicated to eliminating racism, empowering women and promoting peace, justice, freedom and dignity for all.

Saint Paul Police Department's
(GRIP) Gang Reduction Intervention Program

Website: www.stpaul.gov/departments/police

About: To promote safe and healthy neighborhoods through strong, professional partnerships with those we serve in our diverse community.

Five Stone Media and The Turnipseed Project

Website: www.fivestonemedia.com

About: "Transforming lives through media by telling authentic stories of redemption."

Life Rebuilders

Website: www.lrbmn.org

About: Life Rebuilders is a Christian based organization that provides short-term and long-term housing and care solutions for men who have been released from prisons, treatment centers or who are homeless.

Epilogue

From the co-writer:

As part of my work in preparing this book for publication I was honored to spend some time with the men and women whose stories were included.

On a beautiful October afternoon I parked in front of Kiowa's house. He drove up behind me, his son asleep in the backseat of his truck, and I followed him down the block to his sister's place. After his son was ushered inside, we drove off for a late lunch. We were the only ones at the Chinese restaurant just off the highway, and - over a mountain of fried rice - we talked. He explained how self-destructive patterns led to his visiting Tom's trauma center. He told me the experience changed him; gave him renewed energy to move forward. He is still hard at work in his neighborhood, helping with landscaping projects and fixing cars.

I spoke with Caitlyn on the phone. She spoke of the time after the accident as 'her miracle,' and told me how well her body had healed. Like Kiowa, the experience had changed her life and she had become grateful for it. It had opened her eyes and put her on a better path. We spoke about her job and her hope for the future. And then she had to go because she had an appointment to check out a crib. She was going to need one soon. Two years ago she was essentially dead for over an hour - but today she is expecting a baby.

It was an unseasonably warm Thursday morning when I knocked on the door of Tay's house. He welcomed me inside and invited me back into the dining room. He had been eating some ice cream and returned the container to the freezer. He was doing great - like Caitlyn he was completely healed. He spoke warmly of John Turnipseed and told me the greatest lesson he learned from him: Don't get frustrated by life's roadblocks, but find a way around them. To that end he was just offered a new job and was excited to start the next day.

I called Brad on a Sunday night. He wears a brace on his leg and has some loss of function, but he considers himself at 100%. He spoke with energy and humor and is working to translate those skills into becoming a motivational speaker.

Andy and I talked on the phone. It was the end of his workday and he was looking forward to spending time that evening with his daughter. His descriptions about his short experience in jail were colorful, compelling, and filled with the kind of details writers love.

Nada invited me into her home. She is 92 now, but still lives on her own and is sharper than I am. She insisted on making me coffee and giving me homemade baklava as she told me her story. Before I left she dug a box out of a back room and proudly showed me her Emmy.

All of them had a spark, a light inside them, a love for life and a hope for the future. All of them had been touched by the healing power of God. I left their company or hung up the phone energized and enthusiastic about humanity. In their own specific way, they each glowed.

-Brian Scott

Dear God my Healer,

You teach us to "Give thanks in all circumstances." You don't tell us to give thanks FOR the circumstances necessarily, but IN them. With this in mind, today I give You thanks for walking alongside me on the journey that created this book.

Thank You for coming to me on my own terms in ways in which I could understand. Thank You for books and lectures, radio broadcasts, and music.

Thank You for Caitlyn, Eric, Keyonte, Kiowa, Brad, Nada and Andy. Thank You for bringing our story into Yours.

Thank You for sending angels to walk with me; angels in my sister and brother, Amy and Joe; angels in my mother and father, two parents I wouldn't trade for all the world; and angels in two special parents, Bonnie and Don.

Thank You for the miracles I get to see every day at work. Thank You for the thousands of patients I have seen over the years, for the honor of their trust. They are the fuel that keeps me going.

Thank You for my Pastors: Justin and Karl, Rob and Dave, Davey and Topper.

Thank You for a gym in which to find refuge and healing. Thank you for Corey, the owner, and for great work out buddies: Matt, Ben, Kelsey, and Paul. They may call me G-Pa Blee but I can still take take them in a push up contest.

Thank You for safe havens for my family in places like

Lutsen, Mille Lacs, and northern Wisconsin. Thank you for blessing me with good friends like the Dilleys, the Barretts, the Sportels, and Beth and George Snyder.

Thank You for instructors named Craig Groeschel, Rob Ketterling, Chip Ingram, John Bevere, Susie Larson, Max Lucado, Chuck Swindoll, Greg Laurie, Rick Warren, Colin Smith, and Charles Stanley.

Thank You for musicians like Cole Swindell, Jason Aldean, and Rascal Flatts. Through them You often whispered to me "You should be here" at "My kinda Party" and then I will give you a "Rewind."

Thank You for bringing me these men and women who became champions for LIFEteam: Tim Clark, Julie Grengs, John Turnipseed, Mike and Kara Johnson, Mark Bierle, Steve Johnson, Linda Yde, José, Joy, and Jessica, Beth, Tracy, and many more.

Thank You for mentors. Thank you for John Hanson, John Turnipseed, Art Erickson, Stan Hill, Dr. Tom Cogbill, and Dr. David Dries.

Thank You for my own ragtag group of nut-balls in the United Lutheran Beer and Banter men's group. You can't make this stuff up!

Thank You for allowing me to work with one of the finest police departments in America. Please continue to bless and protect the officers of the Saint Paul Police department and their Gang Unit. Thank you for Commander Jon, Sergeant Mark, and John O. Those guys are amazing, God!

Thank you for a wonderful hospital which supports my work from the front door to the back. The talent and compassion of my staff are awe inspiring. Grant a special blessing, God, to the best nurses anyone can find - in Saint

Paul and Red Wing both.

Thank You for the most amazing group of young men and women in Saint Paul. Help both the East Siders and West Siders know how valuable they are in Your sight. Inspire them to come together in peace.

Thank you for my front line workers in Saint Paul. My Boom Girl, Alicia and friend Cha Cho. Thank you for Zach Tift and Otis Zanders; for Richard and Kedar; for my brother in Christ, Joe Lash. Those guys are saints!

Thank You God for blessing me with two sons, Nick and Jack. One gentle and one boisterous - both amazing young men. They have been a gift.

Thank you God for Sondi. I pray for continued healing in our relationship in whatever way You want it to be.

And finally, thank You God for Joy Noel Ashley, my sister from New York. Through her, You showed me how prayer works in a hospital. What my team couldn't fix, You have now healed. Receive her into the loving arms of your mercy.

In Jesus name I pray. Amen.

About the Author

Doctor Tom Blee is a trauma surgeon in Saint Paul, Minnesota. He is the creator and co-director of LIFEteam, a hospital-based intervention program which brings transformational change to those caught in cycles of violence or despair.

The Co-Author

Brian Scott is the author of one previous book, the Christian thriller, <u>That Day, Great and Terrible</u>. He lives in Red Wing, Minnesota with his family.

62678213R00086

Made in the USA
Lexington, KY
15 April 2017